SUSAN ABISHARA

IS THIS THE END OF AGILITY?

WHO WANTS TO BE FAST AND ADAPTIVE ANYWAY

'It is not the strongest of the species that survives,
nor the most intelligent that survives.
It is the one that is the most adaptable to change.'

CHARLES DARWIN

Acknowledgements

To my many children,
adopted and birthed
#Slay
Thank you for keeping me grounded at all times!
Julius, Claudia, Alessia, Billy, Cass, Callie, Sammy

To my bro and sis in law
Love u always

To my book coach,
Andrew Griffiths
Who taught me the importance of not being beige

To all my colleagues and friends
Thank you for going on this journey with me
For providing feedback and keeping it real and honest at all times
Thank you for proving that there is goodness in all organisations
It just needs a light shone upon it – let's shine that light together

And, last but not least, let's not forget
My six turtles, my snake-like, long-necked babies
Who roam the house constantly and cause me daily angst
As I have to count them continually to ensure I haven't lost one

A catalogue entry for this book is available from the National Library of Australia.

ISBN: 978-1-922764-72-0

Printed in Australia by McPherson's Printing
Book production and text design by Publish Central
Cover design by Pipeline Design

Images on pages 34, 53, 58, 77, 93, 99, 109, 120, 132, 144, 154, 187, 209 and 217
© Shutterstock

Disclaimer: The material in this publication is of the nature of general comment only, and does not represent professional advice. It is not intended to provide specific guidance for particular circumstances and it should not be relied on as the basis for any decision to take action or not take action on any matter which it covers. Readers should obtain professional advice where appropriate, before making any such decision. To the maximum extent permitted by law, the author and publisher disclaim all responsibility and liability to any person, arising directly or indirectly from any person taking or not taking action based on the information in this publication.

CONTENTS

Introduction   **1**

Do you want a fast and adaptive organisation?   1

Is agile dead?   3

Being fast and adaptive is essential   6

About agility   6

What lenses should you use?   7

From oil tanker to speedboats   9

My relationship with this well-worn topic   14

Why write another book on this topic?   19

The real opportunity   21

Who is this book for?   23

What problems will this book solve for you?   25

What is the ultimate benefit of reading this book?   25

What actions should you take when you read this book?   26

Advantages of this book   27

Pay it forward – 100% of book profits donated   28

Chapter 1: Is this the END of agility – what went wrong?   **31**

Is this the beginning of the end?   33

What's in a name?   35

How did we get here?   37

Don't get caught in the agile holy war   40

When the wheels fall off   43

Common implementation mistakes   44

Agile – 'something to embrace' or 'just a fad'?   48

Understanding the hype curve and how it applies to agile   49

Not the end, just the trough of disillusionment   52

Chapter 2: WHO has achieved agile mastery and what do they do differently?   53

What do agility masters do differently?   55
What can we learn?   57
Microsoft Corporation   59
Google (Alphabet)   61
7-Eleven Japan   63
Bosch Power Tools   65
LinkedIn   66
Ericsson   68
CH Robinson   69
Barclays Bank   70
BMW   71
Spotify   72
US Federal Government   73
Will agility guarantee success?   75
So, remind me – what did the agility masters do differently?   75
Okay, are you going to show me how to achieve some of
these things?   76

Chapter 3: WHAT is agile and how will you know if you have achieved it?   77

Is your organisation agile?   79
Agility pulse check   79
Agility fitness test   80
Implementing the agility test   86
Custom designing your agility journey   87
Common agile implementation pitfalls   88
Managing the change process   89
The starting line   90

Chapter 4: Putting the WHY into your journey   93

Every journey must start with WHY   95
Agility is a critical business enabler   96
Connecting agility to business growth   97
How to put the WHY into your agility journey   98

Chapter 5: HOW – Getting started on agility — 99

Time to make your organisation agility fit — 101
Outcomes (organisational agility muscle group #1) — 102
Behaviours (organisational agility muscle group #2) — 104
Mastery (organisational agility muscle group #3) — 106
Time to work out! — 108

Chapter 6: HOW – Outcomes first, fast and frequent — 109

Workouts to build your Outcomes agility muscle group — 111
Impact – INSPIRE with a north star — 112
iMpact – MEASURE what matters — 122
imPact – PROVE don't assume — 133
impAct – ACCELERATE time to value — 139
impaCt– CADENCE, fast and frequent — 148
impacT– TRANSPARENCY — 153
Your outcomes muscle group is now fitter and stronger — 160
Behaviours change cultures — 160

Chapter 7: HOW – Behavioural-led culture — 163

Why we need to change behaviours — 165
Workouts to build your Behaviours agility muscle group — 169
Faces – Make FEEDBACK normal — 171
fAces – ACCOUNTABILITY with radical candour — 176
faCes – Healthy CONFLICT management — 180
facEs – ENERGY multipliers and drainers — 187
faceS – SELF-Awareness — 190
Your Behaviour muscles are now fitter and stronger — 193

Chapter 8: HOW – Building a continuous learning organisation — 195

Why we need organisational mastery — 197
The four stages of competence to achieve mastery — 198
The four levels of learning — 200
A continuous self-learning organisation — 206
Agile certification path — 207

Chapter 9: You MADE it   **209**

Is this the end of agility?   211
The time for change is now   212
Let's get started   213
How is your relationship with AGILITY feeling now?   213
What's the path forward?   214

Who am I?   219
Please share your stories and experiences   221
Do you want to share my energy at your organisation?   223
Resources   227

INTRODUCTION

DO YOU WANT A FAST AND ADAPTIVE ORGANISATION?

Honestly, who doesn't? Have you tried to achieve it and failed? And has it left a bad taste in your mouth? Has this failure made your organisation recoil, and pushed you back to your old ways of working? If the answer is yes, don't worry – you are not alone. Corporates globally are feeling this pain. Like all transformative journeys, change takes time. There are no silver bullets, and perhaps the failure upfront is an essential part of the journey, because it forces a 'jolt', a realisation that anything worth achieving is not easy to achieve.

Think of it like any fitness journey: you don't go from not being a runner to running a marathon without ups and downs. When you are in the middle of this journey it may seem like a bad idea – your knees hurt, it's cold outside and no matter what changes you make you aren't getting any faster. Giving up doesn't solve the problem or make you feel any better. Discipline, focus, listening to your body, assessing your progress and understanding your problem areas, as well as taking advice from people who have done it before will make a difference.

The rewards are worth it, but surely there must be a better way?

There has to be a better way – right?

Yes – there is a better way: you need to take a step back. Sometimes you need to go backward to go forward. Pushing through with pure stubbornness is not always the right path; sometimes you must examine the path you are on and why you started down this way to see if it still seems like the right direction. Perspective is important.

This reflection, like all reflection, starts with 'why'. Why did you go down this path to begin with? What were you hoping to achieve? Have you made any progress? How do you know? Is the progress obvious?

1

The 'fast install' button doesn't exist

When I told a good friend of mine I was writing a book on agility and she said, 'Ahhhh, a framework book', I knew it was time to add my voice to this conversation.

There is no framework that will make you a fast and adaptive company. There are many tactics you can try that may or may not work, but being fast and adaptive is much more than a framework. What works for one organisation may not work for another – you need to be prepared to try different things. Frameworks are all about the How; they completely miss the What, Why, Who. How is an important ingredient, but without the other parts it will be meaningless and lack purpose.

Fast and adaptive is not the endgame

While I'm passionate about enabling organisations to be fast and adaptive, I know it's not the endgame. Far from it. Your journey must have a goal and a destination, a purpose, a reason to set out in the first place. This purpose will keep you energised and focused when the going gets tough. Fitness and suitability are critical for all journeys, but there are different types of fitness depending on the destination. There is no point lifting heavy weights five days a week if the goal is running a marathon. Fitness must be relevant to the goal and suitable for the journey to achieve the goal. The tactics you use matter – different tactics work better for different journeys. Choose wisely. If you don't, you may never achieve what you set out to do.

Will agile make my organisation fast and adaptive?

The simple, honest answer is 'maybe'. There are no guarantees. However, I can guarantee it will give you a greater likelihood of survival. You should be okay with that. Surviving in today's market is hard. There are no silver bullets – agile most certainly isn't one. If you tie being fast and adaptive to a business outcome or purpose, you have a greater chance of success because agility is only a means to an end. Then you can measure if it is actually helping you achieve that success or not.

Agility can help you achieve business growth. It is a key ingredient in strategic execution, but there are many tactics, so 'fit for purpose' is key.

Agility is about flexibility; if something doesn't work, then stop using it and try something else. However, make sure you are assessing it for success and understand how you are measuring success. For example:

· Are you using evidence or opinions?
· Have you given it enough time or are you pivoting too early?

These are important questions that will pop up time and time again.

IS AGILE DEAD?

People who have failed on their agility journey will cry, 'Agile is dead!' I wanted to write a book that acknowledged the heated agile arguments rather than ignoring them. There is a lot we can learn by understanding how we got here. History always has a lot to teach us. Agile is no different. Anyone who is a true agilest knows the foundations of agility are transparency, inspection and adaption. So we *must* encourage transparency on failures and inspect them so we can understand them, and rebuild and adapt for the better.

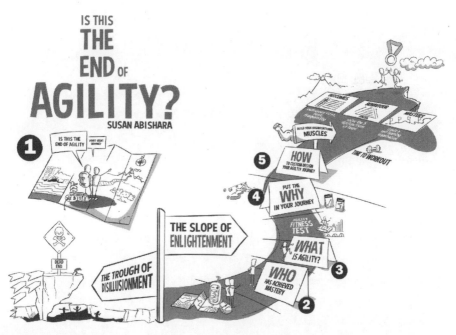

DON'T FOLLOW THE PACK, CUSTOM DESIGN YOUR AGILITY JOURNEY FOR ORGANISATIONAL SUCCESS

We need to stop following without questioning

I want this book to be a thought-provoker for people. I want both sides to stop and pause with curiosity. I want people on both sides to consider the questions. Too many people who are passionate about agile are guilty of blindly following and supporting it, regardless of what success they are having. We need to encourage more critical thinking and debate. Different opinions are *good*, not bad. It's only then that we are truly listening and can take agility through its next maturity curve.

The question 'Is this the end of agility?' is explored in five key parts:

1. Is this the END of agility – what went wrong? (*Chapter 1*)
2. WHO has achieved mastery and what do they do differently? (*Chapter 2*)
3. WHAT is agility and how will you know if you have achieved it? (*Chapter 3*)
4. WHY you need it – business growth and innovation. (*Chapter 4*)
5. HOW to do it – rebuilding and future-proofing your organisation using targeted agility tactics. (*Chapters 5 to 8*)

Let's briefly introduce these topics now.

1. Is this the end of agility – what went wrong?

I want to explore why people would shout 'agile is dead' at conferences. I want people on both sides of the debate to listen and accept that the opinion is a valid one, and that ignoring the opinion will not make it go away. I also want to remind people what the word stands for and to reclaim the word 'agile' so that agile at work represents the English dictionary definition of the word. I want people to question, is my organisation really agile? Should it be agile? What will we gain by introducing this enabler? I want to explore agile against the Gartner hype curve to provide perspective on where we are in the cycle, what stages we have gone through, and what stage is next to help people understand this is a common pattern for innovations.

2. Who has achieved mastery and what do they do differently?

I have come to realise that lots of people talk about agile but most don't actually know what it means. I want to dedicate some time to the subject on what it *is* and what it *isn't*. I want to walk through examples of what successful agile organisations are doing right. I want people to understand what sets these organisations apart so they can be role models for success. I share these examples so organisations can look to these experiences to role model 'good'. I want to share what organisational characteristics these organisations share, so you can learn to recognise if your organisational agility program is achieving agility or if you need to course correct. I want to help organisations see through the noise and have success on their agility journey.

3. What is agility and how will you know if you have achieved it?

I give you a simple definition of what agility is from an organisational perspective, as well as providing an agility fitness assessment you can use to baseline the start of your journey, so you can measure progress. This fitness test will help you pinpoint weak areas in your organisation. You can then use this assessment to create a custom-designed agility journey for your organisation. In exploring what agility is and how to assess your agility fitness, we will also explore the common mistakes organisations make when starting their agility journey. Creating awareness of the most common potholes on an agility journey can help you sidestep them.

4. Why you need it – business growth and innovation

Organisations frequently go wrong by launching an agile transformation program without a why. Agility is closely tied to enabling business growth and helping organisations evolve, accelerate and scale, so they can outperform their competitors. If your agile program is not helping you with this, you need to course correct and do things differently. Your agility program should be tied to real, tangible business objectives. If it is not helping you win in the market or has not delivered proven business results, change it! Stop accepting second-class outcomes.

5. How to do it – rebuilding and future-proofing your organisation using targeted agility tactics

Organisations are more likely to have greater success on their agility journey if they get more targeted. People seem to think agility is 'one big thing' – it's not! It is many tactics that help you with different problems. Becoming more targeted will help people understand what agility is and how to leverage it for success, and ensure they do not get distracted rolling out a big framework.

BEING FAST AND ADAPTIVE IS ESSENTIAL

This is book is designed to show you that being fast and adaptive is essential for your organisational success, and agility can help you achieve it. I want to rewire your understanding of what agility is and how to achieve it. I have 30 years' experience and I can help you recognise real agility, and help you decide if you need to course correct and, if so, the best way to do that.

ABOUT AGILITY

So, if fast and adaptive are essential for business success, what is the best way to achieve these? We need to start with 'What is agility?' So many people have assumptions on what it is – that are often wrong. There are so many heated opinions on such a simple word. How could one word have so many meanings, all conflicting?

Agile is certainly topical. Google returns 344 million references! Sharing with others that you are a passionate agilest will immediately divide the room like the red sea. People will either vehemently agree with you or argue with you. Yes, it would seem these days that bringing agile into a conversation is as divisive as religion and politics. Who would have thought that a term coined over 20 years ago by a bunch of developers would have such an impact? It reminds me of the quote, 'There is no such thing as bad publicity'.

Agile coach ≠ Agility

The next eye-opener that people struggle to accept is that while I am a passionate agilest with 30-plus years' experience, I have never been:

- an Agile Coach
- a Scrum Master
- a Ways of Working Chapter Lead.

Quite simply, none of these things will guarantee your organisation agility. I share this because I want you to think about agility differently and spend time trying to understand it and recognise it. If you want to get a different result and differentiate your organisation from the herd, you need to think about it differently. This is the critical starting point. I share this not to bash agile coaches – I have many good friends who are good at this role. I share this because I don't want you to assume agility and coaching go hand in hand. Sometimes they do, sometimes they do not.

Agility to me is just a set of tools in my toolkit – one of many sets and definitely not the only one. I deliver business outcomes and I use agility tactics to get there quickly and cheaply with happy teams.

WHAT LENSES SHOULD YOU USE?

So to learn more about organisational agility, there are a few lenses to use:

- **Agility inspiration:** The word 'agility' comes from the physical world.
- **Agility foundations:** The concept is based on empiricism, as is modern science and medicine.
- **Agility organisational vision:** Agility can be applied to your organisation, and used when designing and future-proofing your organisation.

It is worth dedicating time to understanding the word from multiple perspectives. This is critical for success. It will stop the blinkered approach of just following what is put in front of you. You will need to critically analyse at each stage of your journey, and these different lenses will be your guide and will help you spot a journey that has gone off track and needs to be course corrected.

Agility inspiration – the physical world

'Agility' is a word from the physical world, often associated with fitness and the ability to move quickly and change position of the body with speed and accuracy. In the sports science community, Sheppard and Young gave agility a fresh description: 'The ability to change velocity or direction in response to a stimulus'. It is influenced by multiple factors, including balance, strength, speed and coordination. Agility is considered a key component of any high performance and fitness. This is what you are trying to recreate in your organisation.

Agility foundations – empiricism

Agile foundations and concepts are based on empiricism. Empiricism states that all learning comes from experience and observations, not opinions and theory. It is the central concept in science and modern medicine: prove your theory using experimentation, and ensure all conclusions are based on evidence.

Empiricism philosophy can be traced back to Aristotle. It became more popular in the 17th and 18th centuries via Frances Bacon, John Locke and David Hume.

'Prove don't assume' – the cornerstone to science and medicine (thankfully!)

The science and medical worlds heavily emphasise the use of experiments and observation to collect evidence and draw conclusions. The goal of experimentation is to apply theories to real-world observations, record the findings as data and utilise them in the real world.

Are you using empiricism in your organisation today? Why not? Organisations that are run as bureaucracies and hierarchies frequently have leaders in charge who think they know better, that their opinions are always right. How many projects have gone wrong because the leader or sponsor assumed their opinion was right and they did not validate it? Many, I would say.

Is your organisation evidence-based or opinion- and theory-based?

The challenge to organisational leaders is this: if your opinion is so right, you should be comfortable having it tested with experimentation and backing up its execution with evidence. The most successful organisations today have moved away from opinion-led decision-making and moved to evidence-based decision-making. This is a cultural shift at the top. Is your organisation ready to make this journey? You may decide you do not need it or want it. That's fine – it is your choice – but remember you will be competing against organisations that decided to bring in the scientific method to allow them to get focused on business results.

Organisations that make their teams commit too early to a set of paper assumptions that are unproven and get disappointed when they don't deliver are setting themselves up for wasting precious dollars.

Agility organisational vision

If you are rolling out an 'agility framework' that is untested in your organisation, you are violating empiricism. Or you may have tested it in one way and proven it, but then applied it organisation-wide thinking that was enough. This is like having medicine for one purpose but using it for another purpose – it's still unproven in the other cases. Evidence that your agility framework will actually deliver success in your organisation is frequently missing when organisations wish to 'go agile'.

Prove what you are doing works with evidence or keep changing it until you can prove it works. This is the essence of agile, and modern life to be honest. Organisations who mandate 'agile' without allowing people to test it and see that it works are destined for failure.

FROM OIL TANKER TO SPEEDBOATS

Agility is about breaking big problems into smaller problems. The oil tanker and speedboat analogy is a common and useful one. Organisations that are like oil tankers are slow to move and change direction, while speedboats can change direction quickly and easily. Speedboats are also viable 'crafts' by themselves.

Big problems to small problems

If I take an 'oil tanker' organisation and change it into multiple speed-boats, how I view the organisation changes. But I don't just take the cargo from the oil tanker and place it on a speedboat; it will sink. How you break up the organisation matters. Speedboats carry smaller cargo and they are autonomous; they can start the journey when they are ready; they can move in any direction they want. They are not tethered to each other. If I was to tether them, I might as well keep the oil tanker.

Speedboat navigation

Each speedboat has a crew, fuel, a starting position and a destination. They have dashboards with a GPS and other instruments that tell them how much fuel they have used, what speed they are going, how far away their destination is. They have a weather app so they can keep an eye on the conditions. They have a radio to keep in constant communication so they can let others know how they are going and if they need help. All decisions are evidence-based – there is no, 'I will provide my opinion on how much fuel we have left', or, 'I will provide my opinion on what speed we are going'. Using opinion rather than evidence would be ridiculous. Everyone on the boat has a role. They help each other where required and they all have access to the dashboard and know how to read it and understand it.

So how do you bring this analogy to life in your organisation? It's worth spending time considering it. For example, if you have one organisation with different lines of business meeting different customer needs, you could make each line of business a speedboat. Remember that speedboats are not tethered and have everything they need.

Deciding what is a speedboat is important ... if one speedboat sinks it should not affect the other speedboats. The lines of business should be P&L focused and the work done should be validated using evidence to see if it had a tangible impact on customers, business revenue and profit. The speedboat should use evidence to validate that they were going in the right direction. They need to be in constant communication with the other speedboats and people on the land.

I share this example for a reason. I frequently see organisations set up tribes and crews as their way of making speedboats out of an oil tanker; however, this is frequently done by HR from a people perspective without understanding the system and technology landscape and the flow of work. Speedboats are set up but they are still tethered together because of technology constraints and workflow constraints. If a speedboat cannot move by itself and is anchored to all the other speedboats, it is still an oil tanker. There is no fast and adaptive oil tanker.

Signs that you are an oil tanker

How do you know if you are an oil tanker or a speedboat? Some characteristics that indicate you are an oil tanker are …

Fixed strategy	Fixed multi-year strategy instead of emergent strategy. Paper-based with a set of unvalidated assumptions. Not a strong relationship with execution of the strategy.
Committing too early	Using a long, laborious business case process.
Big bets instead of small bets	Asking teams to commit upfront when the least amount of information is known, so assumptions are guesses and these guesses are treated as facts. Disappointment ensues when those assumptions prove inaccurate. Teams are blamed, but they were not set up for success.
Slow decision-making	Centralised decision-making, separated from the work being done. This approach slows down teams considerably. Also, it means the people making the decisions are too far from the work and the impact. Constant back and forth asking more questions, so a team can wait months for a decision. Decisions based on politics and opinions rather than evidence.

Everything is important	You want more, not less.
	Everything is rated high rather than ranked in priority order.
	Teams' queues overflow, leading to burnout as there is no consideration for capacity.
	This is an absence of decision-making, usually due to fear of making the wrong decision and forcing everything to the team to complete, resulting in the team seeming to have an inability to deliver rather than it being a lack of prioritisation. This is shifting blame.
People are unhappy	People are seen as expendable.
	Restructures are common, leading to change fatigue.
	There is a constant worry about job security, with honesty and psychological safety being an issue.
	People do not share their concerns as this will have the potential to put them on the next restructure list.
Being internally focused rather than externally focused	Most of the time and energy in your organisation is spent internally rather than looking into the market and assessing conditions, customers, competitors. You think what you offer in the market is unique and cannot be matched and, therefore, you cannot be toppled.

Signs that you are a speedboat[1]

'If you are good at course correcting, being wrong may be less costly than you think, whereas being slow is going to be expensive for sure.'

JEFF BEZOS

Emergent strategy	Shifting to an emergent strategy and constant questioning.
	How do we add value and validating? Strategy and execution are iterative and linked.

Unleashed decision-making	Changing how your organisation operates, moving away from big bets to small bets and fast decisions, and failing small over failing big. Putting decisioning with the work, not multiple steps removed.
Being people-centric	People are your biggest asset and cost – don't hire people and not inspire and motivate them. What a waste! Respect their careers and their desire for mastery, don't ignore them. Richard Branson summed it up so well: 'Train people so well that they can leave. Treat them so well that they won't want to.' Who doesn't value their most expensive asset?
Leadership	Move away from command and control to influencing, and enabling over fiefdoms. Why hire people for what they can bring to the table and then only listen to a favoured few who have a vested interest in the status quo?
Simplicity	Less is more.
Technology savvy	Stop ignoring technology. It is 2023 not 1973 – become digitally savvy for success. CEOs and organisations who fear technology will get left behind.[2] There is no future where technology is not a key ingredient. Putting your head in the sand on the topic is putting your organisation at risk.

*

I share these different lenses on agility to get you to think about the topic a bit more. To understand it, you need to look at it in other environments before applying the lens to your organisation. I will dive further into this topic and teach you to better recognise it in your organisation. We start here because most people simply do not have the right understanding of what agility looks like.

Don't go wrong on the first step of your agility transformation by simply not understanding what the word means and, therefore, incorrectly applying it to your organisation.

MY RELATIONSHIP WITH THIS WELL-WORN TOPIC

So, we have spent some time taking a step back and understanding what agility is. Before I take you on the rest of the journey, I need to share who I am and why I am suited to guide you on this journey to fast and adaptive.

With over 30 years' experience, I will start you with the vanilla LinkedIn version of what I do. This is just so you can anchor what you hear and understand the context that my experience comes from. I specialise in four key areas. These areas are the 'glue' of organisations:

- digital
- organisational health and performance
- agility
- strategic execution.

I am a senior executive leader, an experienced practitioner with proven results, achieved with a focus on ROI and reducing time to market across a wide range of organisations, big and small, and industries (primarily financial, digital, marketplaces, telecommunications and energy). My favourite roles are those where I have the ability to make a difference, rather than those with organisations that are looking for someone to keep the status quo. I am a changemaker; I enjoy this role most. I very rarely use a cookie-cutter approach. I understand that each organisation has its own unique DNA requiring a 'fit for purpose' operating model to deliver and optimise results. I have a wide range of tactics in my toolkit, and I leverage best-in-class methods to help deliver enterprise-wide business outcomes across lean, agile, systems thinking, value streams, devops and service design. My unique approach is people-centric with a focus on cultural and behavioural change and behaviours that create high-performance teams. I believe in creating an environment that is fun, with mutual support in a high-trust model with a high sense of purpose and clarity. An organisation where people find joy in their work is an organisation that has everyone working together for success.

I am hands on, which means it's my responsibility to deliver business outcomes, not just ways of working. I know what works and what doesn't; I have learnt the best way, which is through real success and real failure.

My career journey

Working in pressure environments

My 30-plus-year career started with a computer science degree and many years as a software engineer on the trading floor, building debt derivatives systems for end-of-day trades. Working on the trading floor gave me direct exposure to the highs and the lows of success. I was expected to build solutions to meet complex problems quickly. This was during the '90s, when developers were jacks of all trades. We didn't have project managers, business analysts, testers … we built, tested, collected requirements and supported production environments. We survived, we enjoyed it, I understood how I added value – it was obvious and transparent. I share this because agility ways of working are not new.

Necessity is the mother of innovation

In the early 2000s, I arrived in Australia and started working with a very famous start-up – a tech unicorn that disrupted an industry and won. However, like all successes it was hard earned, and for many years we had to be creative and deliver business results and deal with an organisation that was doubling in size every quarter. A lack of cash in the early years was a godsend; it forced us to be creative in everything we did. We always chose the cheaper solution and kept everything simple and not feature heavy. This was my first (conscious) introduction to agile. The agile manifesto was topical, having been published in 2001, and we experimented and trialled the concept.

Agile to us was many things. We didn't overthink it, nor did we have a grand plan or structure and definitely no framework. We implemented whatever was fast, lean and cost effective, while utilising trial and error. We had great success – enough for me to cement that this fast-and-lean approach was the way forward.

Learning from an agile founding father

I moved back to Europe and London for a few years and I met Ken Schwaber and trained with him. Ken created scrum. I have a personally signed 'scrum licence' from Ken, way before a licence became a 'thing'. My strongest memory was that he was very passionate about commonsense practicality and understanding the essence of what scrum was over a prescriptive approach; short iterations, test and learn.

Enabling speed and diversification

By late 2000s, I had gained confidence in my approach and entered into large-scale agile before the term was even coined. I started a new role, and the organisation's business was dwindling due to changed consumer behaviours. They were aware they needed to change their business model and how they made money, as well as changing how they operated internally. They were slow and bureaucratic, and were keen to pilot an agile approach, which proved successful, delivering more in nine months than the previous three years. This pilot project kickstarted the agility journey for an entire organisation.

Career shift – from technology to business and P&L

Up until now, my entire career was product- and technology-led and this was how I applied agility. I then joined an organisation in a business role and learned to apply agility to sales, marketing, finance, operations and business development, while having P&L accountability for the Australian market. We also ran the organisation on a shoestring, and I enjoyed the challenges of being creative and solving problems quickly and cheaply. I realised that agility is applicable to all aspects of an organisation rather than just technology and product. Our region outperformed all other regions for this organisation (excluding their home market). So we had P&L results that proved our approach was effective compared to other regions globally.

Large scale – successes and failures

In the past few years the success of agile has exploded, which initially made me very excited, until I sampled it with mixed success. After decades of successfully using agile, I didn't recognise what was being rolled out in large organisations. I found it confusing at first. What was I doing wrong? How could I adapt it better? I eventually realised this was not agile at all, and that with mass market adoption people were too quick to embrace something they didn't understand. This created an industry that never existed before of people who did not have the relevant experience guiding organisations that were looking for a silver bullet – which obviously does not exist.

This mass market adoption, along with agile certifications being achieved too quickly and easily, has led to the 'agile is dead' catchcries. To be honest, it is hard to disagree with this. What is being rolled out in a lot of organisations will not achieve success, and a lot have failed already. This was one of the main drivers of this book: to help people recognise *real* agility so they can course correct for a better outcome.

Which brings us to today – how have I managed to achieve success with agility?

I have had to reflect on what gave me the early success with agility that was less prevalent in later years. I think my biggest reflection is that agility is not an entry-level skill, nor is it a skill in isolation. Only when it's utilised with other skills and experience do you get results.

There are four key differentiators worth mentioning:

1. **Technology savvy:** I have worked and built software for decades, hands on, so I am confident working with technology teams and I can speak in simple language so that non-technologists understand how best to apply the technology for business success.

2. **Strategic execution:** I am always surprised by how under-appreciated strong execution and delivery skills in organisations are today. I am going to take a guess this will take on great relevance in future. Most organisations fail today due to poor execution skills. I have spent many years delivering business results – I have seen what works and what doesn't, and I have done every sort of change possible. I can spot an execution problem 10 paces away, purely because I have seen them all a hundred times before, so I can help teams course correct quickly. The biggest challenge is always understanding and defining a good outcome – not as easy as it sounds.

3. **People-centric:** I actually enjoy the company of other people. It helps significantly. A lot of people don't. There is nothing

I enjoy more than watching other people succeed. So I have learnt to foster a positive culture. I firmly believe work can be fun and enjoyable, and that when we have an inclusive, diverse environment where everyone has each other's backs rather than playing a zero-sum game, great successes can be achieved.

4. **Agility and lean, high performance:** I see these as interconnected. I have learned to assess the fitness of organisations and teams using evidence and not opinion, and then to try new things to get into market quicker with a focus on speed and ROI. I will trial many different tactics to make this work, but I always start with a baseline and validate my approach quickly. If it doesn't work, I don't worry – I try something else.

As you can see, I've had a long and tortured relationship with agility and business success. If someone with my experience can get mixed results, can you imagine the outcomes for people with less experience?

This is how I reached the conclusion that it's time to share my experiences with a book. However, there are so many agility 'how to' books; I wanted to take a fresh approach. The challenge today with people working in the agility market is that they refuse to acknowledge there is negativity on the subject. Coming from a group of people who will ask you to embrace continuous improvement and be retrospective, it is almost funny – or sad, depending on your lens. Success in any arena in life requires an honest appraisal of how things are going. Ignoring the negativity will not make it go away. So I decided with this book I would lean into it, embrace it and explain it. That way, you can go into this journey with your eyes open and understand how and where things go wrong, and find a way to sidestep problems.

From this perspective, I draw from many areas of inspiration. They are certainly not all my ideas, but everything in this book I have utilised with success, so what I present here I have personally used in organisations and I share with you what has practically given me great outcomes.

WHY WRITE ANOTHER BOOK ON THIS TOPIC?

To address agile failures

I was reading an article in the *Australian Financial Review* in July 2022. It was this article that prompted me to consider writing this book. It discussed how a large organisation's agile transformation had failed. Another one. Everything about the article made me sad, and the factual inaccuracies grated on me. However, at the same time I can acknowledge that it summed up the market sentiment and the struggle organisations face when wishing to become quick and nimble organisations.

It is time for reflection and debate

So I am writing this book to encourage the discussion on 'is this the end of agility?' I feel this is a conversation that MUST be had, so we can move to the next stage of this journey and provide greater success for more organisations by reframing what agile is and why they need it.

On a daily basis, I hear people share their stories on agile and their experiences and, as I listen, I realise most people don't understand what the word means. The English dictionary definition has not changed. It states, 'the ability to move quickly and easily'. So I want to take them on a journey to understand why some companies achieve fast and adaptive on their agile journeys and others don't.

To help people recognise what is and is not agility

Lots of people are disillusioned by their attempted path to agility. I no longer want to stand by and watch people confuse their poorly executed agility journey with agility 'not working'. The most common assumption people have on agile is that it is daily standups, quarterly planning, sprints, squads and backlogs. This is not agile, and nor is it the ability to adapt and move quickly and easily. This belief is primarily due to organisations liberally using agile as a buzzword internally when they restructure, cut costs and try to invigorate the organisation with a new way of working, but forget to change the political and bullying culture and then wonder why they didn't have success. We need to help agile reclaim its definition of 'the ability to move quickly and easily'.

It's impossible for agility to not be working. The only thing that can be broken is your implementation to achieve agility.

To ensure all agility journeys start with WHY

I want to remind people that their agility journey must have a WHY for success. For organisations, agility can be a critical business enabler for growth and it can help you evolve, accelerate and scale your organisation to outpace your competitors.

There are so many books on 'how to do' agile, but these books preach to the converted. The biggest issues I see on my travels are more to do with *what* agility is and *why* you should do it. *How* is the wrong starting position for most people.

To help organisations achieve agility success by being more targeted

Organisations will have greater success with agility if they became more targeted with their approach. I want to show them what agility tactics to use so they have greater success on their journey to agility.

Preaching to the converted is not enough

A lot of agility books appeal to people who are agile fans. I wanted this book to be different. I wanted it to be topical and to address the 'elephant in the room' of 'is agile dead?' I feel people who hate it have good reason to hate it, and I think we should discuss and understand how we got here. So I would like to appeal to people who are already on the agility bandwagon as well as people who are hesitant or frustrated.

Targeted agility tactics rather than frameworks

The last message I wanted to push home is that I don't reference any agile frameworks and I am specifically agile framework agnostic. Frameworks do not guarantee agility, so I do not wish to distract the conversation on what agility is and how to recognise it. While I do understand why organisations wish to embrace a framework, I show them a different path by giving them targeted agility tactics so they can solve specific business problems rather than follow a framework religiously.

Virtues and pitfalls – both are critical to understand

Most books in this area sprout the virtues of agile while ignoring the pitfalls. For agility to truly succeed, we need to acknowledge the failures and the frustrations people are experiencing, because only then can we lean into improving what agile is to give people a great chance of success.

*

So this book starts with WHAT and WHY before HOW, and provides the history of agile, because only when you understand its history and how we arrived here will you understand how to utilise it more effectively.

THE REAL OPPORTUNITY

True agility

I hope to enable CEOs, senior leaders and organisations to understand what true business agility is, why it's important and how to utilise it as a critical organisational enabler for market and competitive success. However, in doing this, I do not want senior executives to jump in too quickly to their first agile framework and buy it off the shelf (because a friend of theirs from a different organisation is telling them to, for example) and waste millions of dollars.

Pause before starting

So the real opportunity is to pause, reflect and then move forward on your journey to becoming lean, fast and adaptive, with your eyes wide open to the opportunity and the potential pitfalls.

Become fast and adaptive

In today's digital age, fast and adaptive is critical for business success. Old, bureaucratic ways of working are no longer good enough. A company must be lean to survive. For a lot of CEOs, throwing away the rulebook of what got them their original success is hard. I get that.

However, evolution is required, and every generation and industry ends up at a tipping point – that point is now driven by technology that changes the game.

Make love not war

The global agility market is fragmented, with a heavy focus on frameworks and a lot of infighting, which simply is damaging agility as a concept and brand. This infighting creates confusion for people not in the industry and doesn't actually help organisations understand what agility is, how it can help them and how to use it to achieve success. I would like to change this narrative and remind everyone that agile is about individuals and interactions, and help them realise that all this infighting is effectively turning people off the concept of agility and is simply a form of cannibalism. We can disagree intellectually and respectfully with others while being inclusive.

Increase your organisational fitness

Agility has the ability to give your organisation the fitness required to survive in this fast-changing world. Technology, the internet and smartphones have revolutionised business, and companies now must move at pace to survive. Your organisation must learn to continuously evolve and change to stay relevant and ahead of the competition.

A critical business enabler

Use agility as a critical business enabler for growth. It will help you see and leverage new opportunities and help you decide and assess quickly and cheaply what is worth pursuing. It will drive focus in your organisation by driving an evidence-based approach.

*

Use this book to accompany you on your journey to fast and adaptive. This book will help you put the WHY into your agility journey and identify what challenges your organisation faces and what specific tactics can help you solve them. This targeted approach will get you to your end destination quicker. Learn how to use proven, targeted tactics for quick-win success.

The real opportunity is to get ahead of the competitive game by transforming your organisation into a fast and adaptive one – and making it an enjoyable journey for everyone who works there!

WHO IS THIS BOOK FOR?

Starting at the top

Transforming an organisation starts at the top. There is no success unless a CEO starts the journey, embraces it and ensures the team embraces it too. So, I write this book for senior executive leaders who understand that the digital age has changed the game of surviving in a competitive market and that success is no longer guaranteed. You are aware that over 50% of all organisations will be replaced in the next 10 years and you want to build an organisation that can survive in this fast-evolving landscape.

Your growth is dwindling

You are ready and hungry to transform into a business that focuses on growth. Your market share is either slowing or reducing and your competitors are getting in market faster with better innovations.

It's time to transform

You know your current organisational model needs to change to succeed in such conditions. A slow-paced, opinion-led, bureaucratic organisation will not succeed in these new conditions. You know you need to rebuild your organisation to harness the power of digital and agility and to become a fast and adaptive growth organisation.

You are unsure on the path forward

You will have either tried agility and failed, or wish to start this journey but are unsure on where to begin.

Beat the current odds of success

This book is for you if you want to help your organisation beat the current odds of success on your agility journey. You understand that blindly following other organisations is a path to disaster. However, at the same time you are keen to understand which organisations have achieved mastery and understand what they do differently. Also, you are curious to understand if you can avoid the most common pitfalls that other organisations fall into.

You passionately believe there is a better path than being another business failure, and understand that there is no organisational win in blaming agile for any implementation mistakes made along the way. You will have realised that survival is dependent on agility as a critical business enabler. This book is not a technical book, and it is designed for technical and business people alike.

If you can answer 'yes' to any of the following questions, this book is for you. Are you a CEO or a senior executive in a medium or large organisation who:

- wants to outperform the competition and accelerate growth?
- is frustrated that competitors are doing everything better and faster?
- wants to transform your slow, bureaucratic operations model?
- is concerned about your current business decline trajectory?
- wants to know what the fuss is about agile?
- is about to embark on an agile transformation and wants to know what *good* looks like?
- is in the midst of an agile transformation – and hates it?

This book is *not* for you if you want to learn how to implement tribes, squads, daily standups, retrospectives, sprints, showcases or backlogs. I have nothing against these, but implementing them will not change your organisation, and I specifically stay away from these items so many people confuse with 'agile'.

This book is for those who:

- want to put the WHY into their agility journey
- have the power to do so.

WHAT PROBLEMS WILL THIS BOOK SOLVE FOR YOU?

This book will end the debate once and for all on whether agile is a fad or should be embraced. It will help executives realise the only path forward is a fast and adaptive organisation that focuses on growth and can adapt quickly to changing market conditions. It will help them figure out how to get there by showing them who has achieved agility mastery and why, and what pitfalls to avoid as they start or continue the journey.

It will help them recognise real agility and how to assess if they are on the right path. It will help them choose the right agility tactics to solve specific business problems to get targeted quick wins.

It will help you:

· learn to recognise what real agility looks like and if you are on the right path
· understand why some companies achieve fast and adaptive and others don't
· avoid the most common pitfalls organisations make on their agility journey
· understand how to use business agility as an enabler that will underpin growth
· assess and understand if your business is growing or stagnating
· assess your organisational capability to evolve, accelerate and scale growth
· use the right agility tactic for the right problem, ensuring targeted, quick success
· embed a continuous learning and adapting organisation
· build happy teams by understanding that agility needs behavioural and habit change to stick.

WHAT IS THE ULTIMATE BENEFIT OF READING THIS BOOK?

The ultimate benefit of this book is to future-proof your organisation. If you are not growing your business, you are stagnating. If you are not trying to be a market leader, you are a market lagger. This book will show you how business agility is a critical enabler for growth and outperforming your competitors.

Learn how agility is the critical business enabler that will help you build an organisation that can:

- **Evolve:** Grow and adjust to changing market conditions.
- **Accelerate:** Work quickly and efficiently to beat the competition.
- **Scale:** Mobilise your people and build a self-learning and adapting organisation.

There is a right way and a wrong way to do your agility journey. Learn to recognise the difference.

This book will help you put the WHY into your agility journey.

WHAT ACTIONS SHOULD YOU TAKE WHEN YOU READ THIS BOOK?

There are three key actions that I recommend you take when reading this book:

- Think about why you want to start an agility journey.
- Learn to recognise the difference between a successful journey and one that will fail.
- Create a direct relationship between agility implementation and business growth.

Think about the WHY

I want you to think about WHY your organisation should start an agility journey. Agility should be helping you achieve business growth by building organisational muscles to evolve, accelerate and scale. If you have already started this journey, I want you to consider if the WHY is aligned with the action you are taking and if you are making progress against your WHY. If not, I want you to change your course of action.

Recognise the difference between good and bad agility journeys

I want you to learn from the agility masters and understand what they have done differently. I want you to understand the common traps organisations fall into and how to avoid them. I want you to take owner-ship of your organisation's agility journey and do it right. I want you to spend time understanding your organisation's unique problems and to then use targeted agility solutions to solve these specific problems quickly. I want you to create a learning organisation so that people and teams can drive the journey themselves.

Tie your agility journey to business growth

I want you to only roll out agility if it helps you achieve business growth and results. Don't do something that is not adding real, tangible value to your organisation. This approach will help you achieve agility success quicker.

So this book is for you if you want to give your organisation a competitive edge by being fast and adaptive. You are aware agility is not a silver bullet and want some guidance on what bits you should use, in what sequence, and why they will add value to you organisation.

ADVANTAGES OF THIS BOOK

As a senior executive who wants to make your organisation fast and adaptive, I am going to guess you are busy in back-to-back meetings all day, so you have limited time to digest a book. Since this is a book on agility and being adaptive, I have designed it so it can fit into a busy schedule. So there are two ways to tackle this book:

- the old-fashioned way – from start to finish
- the 'I am too busy to read' approach – you can dive into specific parts of the book or a specific chapter and read that in isolation.

Simple and easy to read

I have kept the language in the book deliberately simple and tried to stay away from jargon. It is designed to be an easy read rather than heavy going, so you can read in short bursts.

I frequently see leaders in organisations continue with activities because they simply do not have the language to question what is occurring. This book is designed to give you the language and confidence to talk to an agility specialist and to challenge what is being done to ensure a better outcome.

Visual and engaging

So many books on agility are dull, with pages and pages of writing. I wanted to create a book that was visually pleasing, so it would encourage people to browse through it and to come back and read it over and over. I am also aware that most people are visual learners, and for these people visualisations are a key to memory retention. I am also aware that attention spans are not what they used to be, so I created visuals for each chapter.

Enjoyable

Finally, I wrote the book to be entertaining and enjoyable to read. I want to take you on a journey of rebuilding your organisation using agility, and to do that I take you back to the start of the journey as it will affect your path forward.

*

So the best way to get the most out of this book is to read it when you have time, in short, sharp bursts. It is designed to be earmarked and to allow you to easily deep dive into a chapter without having to work your way up to the chapter, because quite simply who has the time to read a full book these days?

PAY IT FORWARD – 100% OF BOOK PROFITS DONATED

I attended school in Ireland in the '80s. Ireland was (and is) a religious state, so boys and girls were segregated for education. As a teenage girl, my school offered no chemistry or physics. We were encouraged to do home economics instead, which I took as a subject. My partner always raises an eyebrow at this, as I am certainly not domesticated nor do I adore cooking – and my family definitely do not adore eating my cooking!

This was obviously a long, long time ago, but I am incredibly disappointed to see that the dial has not moved that much since – only 20% of all computer science undergraduates are female today. I have a teenager daughter and I know full well that representation matters. She does not want to attend classes where she is one of a small number of females.

Research shows diverse teams solve problems better and more creatively. I have frequently heard male senior technology executives say they have tried to solve the gender gap, but the reality is if they wanted to it could be solved within a few years. The gender gap in technology is actually a problem that men must solve. It is not a female problem. We need men in leadership roles in technology to lean in and own it and not take the easy way out and say 'it is too hard' or 'I tried'.

Ways it can be solved creatively include:

· cross skilling from one role in the organisation to a technology role
· training up females with potential and giving them on-the-job training
· sponsoring non-technology graduates interested in solving problems with technology
· ensuring technology focuses on problem-solving not systems.

As a female leader in technology, I care about representation. It matters. It delivers results, and sometimes it requires us to go above and beyond to get a better outcome. I am donating 100% of the profits of this book to charities that encourage young girls and women to take up a career in technology.

Choosing technology has changed my life from a poor working-class suburb in a disadvantaged area in Ireland to living inner city on the other side of the world in Melbourne, Australia. We need to give all young girls the confidence to be brave and step into the unknown and learn the rewards of a career in digital. By purchasing this book, you are contributing also.

Thank you!

CHAPTER 1

IS THIS THE END OF AGILITY – WHAT WENT WRONG?

'THIS IS NOT THE END,
THIS IS NOT EVEN THE
BEGINNING OF THE END,
BUT IT IS, PERHAPS, THE
END OF THE BEGINNING.'

WINSTON CHURCHILL

IS THIS THE BEGINNING OF THE END?

I was eating breakfast one Sunday morning at my local Melburnian, hipper-than-thou coffee shop where all the baristas had beards and tatts and the music was pumping. On the front page of the business section of the newspaper was a story about an organisational transformation. I lapped up every detail, reading the story two or three times. I remember desperately wanting to be part of this 'agile' club. I was in awe of the bravery, going agile enterprise-wide. I wanted to work there. With a career spanning over 30 years (yes, I am old) and 20 years specialising in agile, this sounded exactly like the kind of challenge I was looking for. I became laser focused and eventually landed the job of my dreams!

Life was good.

The first day I arrived was quarterly planning day. I couldn't believe my luck. I would get to see everything in action on day one. The room was massive. There were approximately 50 large A-frame boards with cards covering them. I was overwhelmed by the amount of information and people – it was definitely exciting and fun and everyone was happy. I didn't actually understand anything, but it was my first day, so that didn't bother me. It was a positive day and everyone was super pumped. It was impossible to not get carried away by the energy in the room.

Day two brought with it my first standup. We had a little ball named 'twinky', and you could only talk if you held twinky. The ball got passed from person to person and you provided your update when holding the ball. Again, I couldn't understand exactly what we were working on, but the enthusiasm was contagious and everyone was lovely. I was very happy to be part of this crew.

Six months later, not much had changed. I realised that we performed all these ceremonies that didn't make any sense. Most people agreed, but everyone was afraid to speak up. There was an uneasy feeling of being in a cult or a religion. I was still unsure what the point of our team was. I had come to realise I wasn't the only one who felt that way, but only in very quiet whispers was the most the subject was ever discussed or mentioned, everyone afraid that if they spoke up they would lose their roles. I found the fear confusing. It seemed like a happy, positive place. Why was everyone afraid of losing their job?

Eight months in, I realised this was not what I had expected. I was genuinely confused. I had a long history of working in agile environments, very much focused on doing things quickly and cheaply across big and small companies. During this time, no one told us how we should work. We talked frequently, but we didn't have rituals. If we needed to have a chat, we did, but if everyone was busy and unblocked we left everyone alone. We made our own rules up; if something wasn't working we changed it, and if it was working we left it alone – we definitely didn't overthink it. Our focus was working software, and if it wasn't working it was obvious and we fixed it. We all knew the intent: get something into customer hands quickly and cheaply. I realised in my new organisation, it *looked* like agile, it *smelt* like agile, but it wasn't agile. They had missed the fundamental essence of what it was. In industrialising it, they had focused on the wrong things: new job titles, ceremonies and sticky notes, as opposed to putting stuff into customer hands quickly and cheaply. I also discovered why there was fear of speaking up. The transformation had been proceeded by a restructure where thousands of people had lost their jobs. The fear was real. The people who were left all had friends and colleagues who had lost their jobs, and they were still grieving, albeit hidden behind a smiling face.

For the first time, the 'emperor's new clothes' popped into my head.

WHAT'S IN A NAME?

Luxurious living

Then a moment of inspiration came while I was in a traffic jam on an inner-city street in Melbourne with my son. We were casually chitchatting and my son pointed to the new apartments going up on the corner block. 'Luxury,' he scoffed. I glanced to my right and read the sign on the building: 'Luxury boutique, premium living'. I had to agree with him; they looked like tiny, poor-quality apartments rather than 'luxury'. We drove by three more new developments on the way home, all claiming to be 'luxury' and all looking very non-luxurious. We agreed that there should guidelines for using words like 'luxury' to describe something. It made me reflect on my working life.

Agile fragile

The word 'agile' in enterprises today is like the words 'luxury' and 'boutique' in the property industry. The words have become meaningless. They are overused, purposely manipulated to paint a picture of a situation that was not real, or perhaps in some cases being used without a true understanding of what they mean. These words had quite simply become 'marketing' to paint a false promise.

Agile is dead

Just last week, I attended a conference and one of the speakers stated with confidence agile is dead.

It wasn't the first time I had heard such sentiment. There is anger in the developer community with 'agile' and all the 'constraints' it imposes. I can understand their frustrations. I have similar frustrations. When I tell people I specialise in agile, the next question they ask is, 'Which framework do you recommend?' I always answer that it depends on the situation because there is no one size fits all, and that it's important to not get fixated on frameworks.

So, how is it possible for a word to become so sullied? To remind myself, I Googled 'agile'. The dictionary definition of the word 'agile' is:

Able to move quickly and easily.

Phew! The meaning of this word had not changed in the dictionary.

I like this definition. It makes sense to me. What doesn't make sense is 'agile is dead' – how could the ability to move quickly and easily be dead? Also, when you read the definition, asking someone what framework they recommend does not make sense either. The problem with the word 'agile' is that people have changed the meaning in their own heads, due to marketing messages from others wishing to sell them something. It would seem that the word 'agile' is now confused with the word 'framework'.

This is an apple

Old words, new meanings

To be honest, it is not unusual for words to have changed meaning over time. For 'research' purposes I Googled it (the latest book research tool) and here are some interesting words that have changed their meaning over time:

Word	Original meaning	Current meaning
Silly	Blessed with worthiness	Daft
Flux	Diarrhoea or dysentery	Continuous change
Fudge	Lies and nonsense	Sugary treat
Leech	Doctor or healer	Blood-sucking worm
Stripe	Mark on the skin	Straight lines pattern

Next time my kids call me silly, I am going to remind them it means blessed with worthiness.

How many organisations state they are 'going agile' but don't look or act agile? Most people can talk about what agility is but from a work perspective struggle to turn that definition into reality. The word means too many things to too many people and companies. The most consistent meaning when companies say 'agile' is they really mean 'restructure', sadly.

So, we are at a tipping point with the word 'agile' – do we continue to let organisations state they are agile without asking them to share how and why? Either we protect the original meaning of the word and call out organisations that use it but mean something else, or we accept the word is sullied and start using a new word.

Are you agile? Or is it agility?

This is where the word 'agility' creeps in. Full disclosure: this is my new word of choice when I speak to people (and is used also in the title of this book), *but* I have a lot of mixed feelings about changing to a new word when there was nothing wrong with the old word, agile. However, if introducing a new word makes it easier for people to move past their grievances and also realise there is a difference between the words 'framework' and 'agility', then so be it – let's adopt a new word!

Agile has been a victim of its own success

Language is how we communicate and get things done in groups. Mass confusion occurs when people use the wrong words in the wrong context. Agile has been a victim of its own success. When it went mass market and every organisation decided they needed it, the word lost its meaning, which is a shame. The word is perfect; it is people's poor understanding of the word that is wrong. So the next time someone tells you they are agile, I encourage you to dig a little deeper to see if their meaning is the same as your meaning.

HOW DID WE GET HERE?

Why was agile brought into workplaces?

We just covered how the word 'agile' has too many interpretations, most of them inaccurate. So where did agile come from? Let's go on a history lesson. It is important to understand the origins of agile.

Let's start with why it was created. Technology projects were taking many years to complete and to get into market, because the software industry had become extremely risk averse and they were protecting themselves by requesting that stakeholders document what they wanted upfront. In doing this, software teams were protected if a project didn't deliver the expected results. So from a risk and protection perspective, it worked a treat. However, people are not great at documenting how systems should work on paper. So while this approach protected the software team, it meant projects took a really long time to deliver and frequently didn't meet requirements at the end, either because the market or demand had changed before it came to market or the requirements were documented badly.

A different way of doing things

Developers wanted to deliver something that customers wanted. Can we meet customer need and do it differently, in a shorter time, and allow stakeholders to look at working software? Agile enters the picture. While it was first referenced in 1995, agile came into organisational language in 2001, promoted by a bunch of software developers via the Manifesto for Software Development. They got together for a weekend, skied, drank beer and ate too much, and drafted the manifesto. They all had different practices (scrum, extreme programming) and ways of developing code, and decided to draft a manifesto that represented what had worked and what was the 'essence' of all the different methods they had used successfully. It was designed for small teams.

I am not an agile evangelist, but I am a fan of well-executed agile. I have seen it work, and I have seen it implemented badly and fail. It works when people understand the intent and are flexible in how it's implemented rather than following a rigid framework.

Context matters

I share these origins because context matters. Understanding context will change the course of your journey and help you better understand the destination. In 2001 we were not using smartphones or social media. TV and newspapers were the primary media channels. Physical stores were the primary shopping destination.

Times have changed.

The manifesto was also written to help software developers build better software by sharing principles and concepts they found worked best in their experience. As a manager of software teams, I know that their methods simply work. So, I am an advocate. However, the approach was designed for use with small software teams and not large organisations enterprise-wide. While they were definitely onto something that could be applied enterprise-wide, obviously it was important to apply this knowledge practically by understanding the original intent rather than blindly following guidelines. That was never the intent.

Understanding the intent for success

The intent of agile was agility, which is the ability to welcome and adapt to change quickly and easily. It was to continuously improve, always. So it makes sense that what worked in 2001 in a vastly different time needs to be improved or seen through a different lens of 20 years of change and adaptation.

Agile was never introduced as a rigorous set of rules to be followed for success. That is almost the antithesis of agile. I wrote this book to bring agile back to life for everyone.

Have you actually read the agile manifesto?

You will find the original agile manifesto here: https://agilemanifesto. org. I share this because I am frequently surprised by people who have never looked at it or don't know what it actually is, even though they work in the industry or are in the middle of an agile transformation.

It is not a bible

The lines I want to draw your attention to are:

> We are uncovering better ways of developing software by doing it and helping others do it.

The entire premise of this is continuous improvement. It is not static or fixed. It was designed to be flexible, which is why they described a set of principles rather than a framework. This approach accurately represents the dictionary definition of the word 'agile' and explains why they selected the word to represent what they were trying to achieve.

If you think agile is a framework to be followed, unfortunately you are listening to marketing messages from organisations selling you a framework and a (supposed) silver bullet, or to an organisation that is taking the word and using it to describe their restructure or headcount reduction.

Is it just for technology teams?

Agile was coined in the technology space, so it is most used by technology teams. Basically, they have been using it longer. This does not mean it's only suited to technology teams. You have learned why technology teams introduced it – it was taking too long to delivery anything because technology had become too bureaucratic and risk averse. But these challenges occur in all areas of an organisation. So the next time someone tells you agility is only for technology teams, help them understand that technology teams were simply ahead of the curve, and being fast and adaptive is a critical skillset for everyone in the organisation.

*

I encourage you to understand where agile came from because it will affect how you implement it in your organisation. It will help you see who actually understands it, what it is and why it was created. This is essential. You need to start leaning into mastery for transformation success.

DON'T GET CAUGHT IN THE AGILE HOLY WAR

Back to the future?

Okay, now we have gone through a little history lesson of agile, let's warp-speed forward to today. What has changed between then and now? Well, if we teleported from then to now, you would be confused by the landscape you see in front of you. Agile has become a noisy subject.

My way is better than yours

So, if you are confused about how you should implement agile in your organisation, you are not alone. The agile market is fragmented, with a lot of angry shouting over which approach is better. When I first decided to write this book, I also decided to broaden my reach on LinkedIn. I was curious what was going on in the global agility market. So I reached out to people who I felt had interesting perspectives on agile. I was excited by all the people and content that resonated with me. At the same time, I reached out to one guy in Germany and sent him a request. He was at least kind enough to email me back, but he said we couldn't possibly be linked in connections as I have a SAFe certification on my profile from 2015. He stated that being connected with me would be bad for his personal branding.

Seriously …

The first rule of 'agile club' is …

Individuals and interactions over processes and tools.

So many people who work in agile treat these pillars as inviolable, yet at the same time the same group of people get into heated wars, arguments and name calling when someone wishes to use a framework that is different to the framework they use.

Spin the wheel, pick the right one

There are so many frameworks and approaches out there. SAFe, LeSS, Nexus, scrum, XP, kanban, lean, disciplined agile, systems thinking, theory of constraints. The list goes on and on … I have worked with agile for 20 years and I have seen all of these frameworks work and I have seen them also fail because context matters. If you are using a framework and it works for you, then please continue. If you are not having success, then change it up. It isn't hard. It is simply common sense.

Fit for purpose

What works in a small organisation is different to what will work in a large organisation. What works for an experienced agile team is different to what will work with a less experienced agile team. What will work for a purely technical team is different to what will work for business teams or blended teams. Also, I don't understand why you would limit yourself to one way of working … the goal should be to experiment and try things. Be precise. What is the problem you wish to solve? Utilise a tactic that solves that specific problem.

Don't limit your tactics

When I say I specialise in agile, I use many tactics across a wide range of methods – lean, devops, DORA, canvas, kanban, scientific method, theory of constraints and systems thinking … plus more that I can't be bothered listing because it simply is not relevant. I have no interest in limiting my tactics for success and neither should you. In the future, I will be using different tactics as new ideas and tactics are shared by others, perhaps tactics that do not exist today. I definitely will not be limiting myself or the organisation I am working with. Why would anyone? Use what works. Don't judge other people's journey. You have no idea what works for their environment and how it differs from yours.

Watch out for the cannibals

Think about how crazy the noise is in the market and in the agile community itself. This group of people promote agile as a mindset, yet fight others claiming one method is better than another. These same people promote collaboration yet choose to fight people who do agile differently. They promote a flexible way of work yet are rigid and fixed to what agile is.

If it wasn't so negative, it would be funny. If agile is dead, it's because the community decided to cannibalise itself and made anyone interested in it run away.

There is enough room for multiple approaches. There are so many scenarios different to the ones you have experience in. Be adaptive and flexible! Be agile.

Just so you don't have to Google them

Okay, I will share a range of tactics just to save you the hassle of Googling them … there are at least 30 variants. Here are just a few:

- scrum
- SAFe
- kanban
- lean
- LeSS
- theory of constraints
- systems thinking
- lean start up
- flow
- disciplined agile
- devops
- the Spotify model.

The key message is do not get distracted by the noise in the market. If you want to introduce agility to your organisation, a framework is definitely not the starting position.

Who's wants sauce with their agile?

So, the market is noisy. Everyone is selling their agility wares. Do not listen to anyone who tells you they have the secret sauce and if you roll out their framework, success will automatically be yours. They are not telling the truth, and if you were to think about it you know this. It is just an easy out – don't take it. There are no shortcuts. Put the effort in now. It will be quicker and cheaper in the long run. The agility failures highlight this.

WHEN THE WHEELS FALL OFF

Why are there so many agile failures that have left people scarred enough to call out that agile is dead? There are three key reasons:

- **Not agile:** Most agile transformations are not actually about agile at all, but are about rolling out a framework without ever considering what agile really is and why they wish to embrace it in the first place. Organisations are hoping a framework is a silver bullet, which obviously it isn't.

- **Hidden agendas:** Far too many organisations call their headcount reductions agile. In fact, so many organisations take this path that many people think agile and restructure actually go hand in hand. Organisations do this to hide that they are cutting costs and people are losing their jobs. They focus on positive PR, which is they will become agile. It is simply a distraction.
- **Marketing:** The agile market is lucrative. As mentioned previously, there are many frameworks and many heated arguments about which ones work and which ones don't. Again, unfortunately these consultants forget to tell you that following their framework will not guarantee agility mastery.

I have had direct involvement in and exposure to many agile transformations over the past 20 years. What is most interesting is that the earliest ones were the most successful – when there was less baggage, fewer opinions, and less of a fixed mindset on how you should do agile. There was less push back from engineering teams and everyone was happy to give it a go. My most recent exposure has been across multiple large organisations of over 10,000 people, either as an employee, contractor or consultant, and the recent pattern of how agile is implemented is effectively consistent regardless of size or organisation. This will cause organisations to fail on their first attempt. To be honest, this is okay. Once you have this perspective and understand why it went wrong, you can lean into it being a journey and not a destination.

COMMON IMPLEMENTATION MISTAKES

There seem to be common mistakes that organisations make when they embark on their agility journey. Do any of these look familiar to you?

Rolling out 'cut-and-paste' agile

Each organisation is as unique as a fingerprint and has its own organisational DNA. The DNA is composed of people, organisational maturity and size, successes and failures, technology choices and legacy systems.

Each organisation has different strengths and weaknesses. So rolling out the same agile framework across all organisations will not work. I call this 'cut-and-paste' agile or 'cookie-cutter' agile.

Begin your journey well prepared. Try to understand your organisational DNA before starting. Doing this will give you the greatest chance of success. Custom design your agility journey. Define what success is for you, what problems you want to solve and what problems you are not ready to solve. How can you amplify your strengths and sidestep your weaknesses?

Like all journeys, you must understand your current position before starting; otherwise, you will head off in the wrong direction. If I want to go to Sydney and my starting position is Melbourne, obviously my journey will look significantly different compared to starting from Canberra or Perth. Do not take the same journey as other organisations. They are at a different starting position to you and are most likely off to a different destination.

'Cut-and-paste' agile is:

- **No Why:** Your organisation has not defined what they hope to achieve and what problems are currently standing in the way.

- **No understanding of organisational DNA:** You decide to roll out agile without first understanding your organisation and how it might affect your agile implementation. For example, what is suitable for a non-regulated business is not suitable for a regulated business. Legacy tech assets have different needs to digital tech assets. You must also consider the size and age of your organisation, and skillsets and experience, along with the culture and political landscape.

- **Same framework as everyone else:** You decide to roll out the same framework as another organisation because they stated in the press that it is great.

- **Mislabelling staff reductions:** You call a headcount reduction an agile transformation.

Focusing on frameworks (HOW) rather than outcomes (WHAT/WHY)

As Simon Sinek says, start with WHY

In this common mistake, the focus becomes about HOW rather than WHY you started this journey. Most organisations that start their agility journey latch onto which agile framework they will choose. They commit to the framework too early, usually before testing whether it will work for them, and the focus becomes rolling out the framework to all teams rather than focusing on WHY they wished to start this journey and what business outcomes they had hoped to achieve. A framework is a means to an end, it is not the endgame. Take what parts of it work for you and embrace them. If bits don't work for you, understand why and then change them and improve them.

Organisations get so wrapped up in rolling out a framework and how it works that they forget why they are doing it. This is the wrong focus, and success is then assessed by how you have implemented the framework. Successfully rolling out an agile framework is not success! Rolling out a framework without spending time on WHY will make you fail.

Start with the problem

What you are doing *must* solve the problems that existed before you started; otherwise, you are wasting time, money and energy. Ensure the problems you want solved are getting solved. You must track the problems and how they are changing over time.

Organisations like this frequently have 'agile framework police' – it's true ☺ – and a 'rollout big bang' but these actions are fundamentally the antithesis of agile.

Ignoring behavioural and cultural change

Who loses if the status quo changes?

The biggest stumbling block to agile at your organisation will be culture and behaviour. It is simply impossible to roll out a new way of working without changing people's behaviours and the culture of the organisation.

If you ignore this, you will simply end up in the same position. I know this is logical, but it is frequently ignored. High-performing organisations utilise the brainpower of everyone in the organisation, not just a chosen few who hold the reins of power tightly. Psychological safety and high trust are critical behaviour patterns for success.

The elephant in the room

I have not yet seen even *one* organisation focusing on agile also put any time or energy into cultural change. It is impossible to create a new way of working without changing the environment it needs to grow in. Old habits and norms need to be replaced with new ones. Old politics, hierarchies and fiefdoms need to be acknowledged and changed.

The path to mastery is undercooked

Unlearn first

Learning a new way of working takes time and effort. Frequently this has being described as 'unlearning'. I get this. To learn a new way of working you must unlearn your current way. I think people need to think about this more. What will you unlearn? Organisations must build this learning time into a team's rhythm and cadence for success. All too frequently, organisations send people on a training course and assume learning can be ticked off as achieved, instead of embracing and understanding that learning a new skill is a journey in itself.

Passive learning is not enough

Organisations seem to train people up front and then say, 'Okay, you have enough skills. We will stop working in the old way on Friday and we will start in the new way of working on Monday.' What happens is that people continue working their old way, just using new terminology. They do this simply because they do not know any better and they are confused. I have spent a lot of time embedding new ways of working, so I am aware of how people learn and I have experienced these failures firsthand. The statistics are that 90% of what is learned is forgotten one week after a training course. Also, it is impossible for a team to do something well without first seeing what 'good' looks like. Role modelling 'good' is important so that people can watch, learn and understand what they need to mimic to get it right. Organisations severely underestimate how long it can take people to learn.

*

So, are you and your organisation going to be another statistic in the agile failures? Or will you do it differently? How will you know what path to pick? When will you know if it is the right one? These are important questions that should be asked the entire way along your journey.

AGILE – 'SOMETHING TO EMBRACE' OR 'JUST A FAD'?

Eyes wide open

With all these failures, perhaps you shouldn't even try? Well, the reason I share the failures is to ensure you go into this journey with your eyes wide open. It isn't to stop you proceeding; instead, it is to explain there are no silver bullets in life and agile isn't one either. I want you to pause and spend time understanding why you wish to start this journey and what you hope to achieve before you get carried away by all the excitement.

A hint of a sniff of success

Plenty of research shows agile organisations perform better. Agile companies, on average, are 1.7 times more successful than their peer group.[3] Agility is seen as a critical business enabler, a competitive advantage and the key to success in a dynamic market.

Agility is also one of the hottest topics in organisations today. A Google search for 'agile transformation' will show you 100 million hits. A recent McKinsey survey shows agility delivers proven business results, with over 70% of agile organisations ranked in the top quartile for organisational health and performance compared with 10% to 15% of non-agile organisations.[4] *Harvard Business Review* has found that most organisations have listed agile as a strategic priority, with more than 8 out of 10 organisations committed to adopting it. More than half are in the process of doing so, and 25% have already put it into practice.

Leave the industrial era behind – it's the digital age

Organisations have not yet embraced that this is about truly transforming a model designed for the industrial era to one suited to an agile organisation that is a growing, learning and adapting living ecosystem in constant flux, in order to exploit new opportunities and add new value for customers. It requires you to think about how organisations operate differently – from fixed to adapting.

This shift of operating model is critical because we are now in the digital age not the industrial age, and the average tenure of organisations in the S&P 500 has shifted from 33 years to 14 years. In fact, it's predicted that this will get shorted further, and over 50% of all companies are predicted to be replaced in the next 10 years.[5]

Do or die

It can all sound a bit dramatic, but a lean, fighting-fit organisation is really the only way to go. Slow, bureaucratic organisations are a dying breed. Kind of like dinosaurs, they were once magnificent and ruled the world for a long time – and then the world changed and they became extinct. Adapt, get fitter and stay competitive in the marketplace.

UNDERSTANDING THE HYPE CURVE AND HOW IT APPLIES TO AGILE

What is the hype curve for innovations?

The best way to answer the question 'Is this the end of agility?' is to look at the journey through the lens of the Gartner hype cycle. Innovations come and go and adapt. Agile is no different. The Gartner hype cycle is a great way to describe the situation agile is in today. It can also help explain why there are divisions in agile.

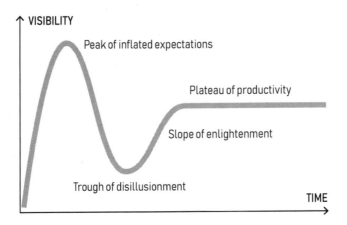

The hype cycle has five defined stages:

1. **Trigger:** A potential innovation breakthrough kicks things off. Early proof-of-concept stories and media interest trigger significant publicity. Often no usable product exists and commercial viability is unproven.

2. **Peak of inflated expectations:** Early implementation and publicity produces a number of success stories – often accompanied by scores of failures. Some companies take action; many do not.

3. **Trough of disillusionment:** Interest wanes as experiments and implementations fail to deliver. Producers of the innovation shake out or fail. Investments continue only if the surviving providers improve their products to the satisfaction of early adopters.

4. **Slope of enlightenment:** More instances of how the innovation can benefit enterprises start to crystallise and become more widely understood. Second- and third-generation products appear from innovation providers. More enterprises fund pilots; conservative companies remain on the sidelines.

5. **Plateau of productivity:** Mainstream adoption starts to take off. Criteria for assessing provider viability are more clearly defined. The technology's broad market applicability and relevance are now clear.

Where is agile on the hype curve?

So let's think about agile from an innovation perspective. I have marked a little arrow in the following figure as to where I think agile is in its innovation lifecycle.

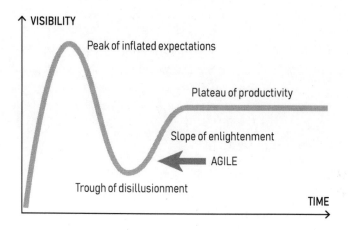

Where is agile?

Innovation trigger? Yes – software development projects were taking too long, were too risk averse and were not meeting customer needs. So agile was invented.

Period of inflated expectations? Yes – lots of organisations have agile as a buzzword in some shape or format, so agile has gone through a period of inflated expectations with a lot of publicity, with successes and lots of failures. Do we have a lot of 'exaggerated' claims of companies claiming to be agile? Yes.

Trough of disillusionment? Well, with some people saying that 'agile is dead' but still having lots of evangelists, I would say 'yes or maybe'. We are either there already, or about to hit it.

So, what is the next stage in the lifecycle of innovation?

Slope of enlightenment. This is when the innovation is starting to become more widely understood. There are second- and third-generation attempts in the market. More enterprises fund pilots; conservative companies remain on the sidelines.

I would say the reframing of 'agile' to 'agility' is the start of the **slope of enlightenment**. The intention of using a new word is to make people pause and ask themselves, 'Why would they change the word?'

NOT THE END, JUST THE TROUGH OF DISILLUSIONMENT

The key message is that the ability to move quickly and easily and adapt to market change can never be dead. Far from it. It's critical to business success, but it must be done properly and – like everything else worth achieving in life – it is hard work that requires focus and discipline, but the benefits are large.

Stop the misconceptions

What needs to be dead is people having misconceptions about what agile is. People must realise these are simply marketing messages from organisations wanting to reduce headcount or make a fast buck.

To move to the next stage of agility, we must acknowledge both sides of the argument and listen. The concerns are valid. We need to work together to resolve them and help organisations learn true agility rather than informing everyone it is a framework.

This is not the end of agility, but instead the trough of disillusionment.

I understand that this can be a frustrating journey, but the starting position to the slope of enlightenment is to find some role models of organisations. Who does this well? How did they do it? What success did they achieve and what can you learn from it?

The next chapter leans into who the agility masters are and what they have done to deserve such a title.

CHAPTER 2

<u>WHO</u> HAS ACHIEVED AGILE MASTERY AND WHAT DO THEY DO DIFFERENTLY?

'IF PEOPLE KNEW HOW HARD
I HAD TO WORK TO GAIN MY
MASTERY, IT WOULD NOT SEEM
SO WONDERFUL AT ALL.'

MICHELANGELO

WHAT DO AGILITY MASTERS DO DIFFERENTLY?

Agility mastery = Greater business results

With all the cries of 'agile is dead' and so many failures, has anyone actually mastered agility? This is the topic of this chapter. The message of this section is that agility success is possible and is tied directly to better business outcomes. However, it must be done properly. We will explore some agility masters, so you can recognise 'good' agile by understanding who the agility masters are, what they do differently and how you can learn from them.

Agility masters have a number of traits in common when compared to the mainstream:[6]

- They are 4.1 times more likely to have the right vision and strategy.
- They are 2.3 times more likely to have a culture to support risk-taking.
- They are 2.3 times more likely to train for continuous skill development.
- They are 2.9 times more likely to have teams skilled in the latest tools and trends.
- They have 60% higher revenue and profit growth than other organisations.

The case for embedding agile broadly throughout your organisation is real and tangible.

The evidence-based research

It is quite hard to get relevant research on agility, but a group of companies formed a consortium to try to do just that, and to share and learn from each other. I love this as a concept – companies opening their doors to others so we can learn together without the worry of confidentiality. Too many companies worry about their IP – which frequently, quite frankly, isn't that special – rather than embracing the benefits of open sourcing from the community. The benefits of open sourcing from others most definitely outweigh any potential risks. Have a think on the risk/reward of doing things differently.

In March 2015, a group of 11 companies formed the Learning Consortium for the Creative Economy.[7] The intent was to explore some questions on enterprise operational models and what approaches were most tied to business success, along with understanding the impact of technology on how business works and if management practices from the twentieth century – such as hierarchy and bureaucracy – were still relevant in today's digital age. They wanted to see if there were patterns across selected companies. The research took the form of site visits to observe how the organisations worked and the impacts on business success.

What is most interesting is that the companies are diverse in age, size and location. The sites visited – and their location and industry – were:

- Microsoft, Seattle, US, technology
- Ericsson, Athlone, Ireland, network and telecommunications
- Riot Games, Santa Monica, US, eSports
- Magna International, Barcelona, Spain, manufacturing
- Menlo Innovations, Michigan, US, software
- C.H. Robinson, Minnesota, US, logistics
- Brillio, Bangalore, India, technology
- SolutionsIQ, Seattle, US, technology services
- Agile42, Berlin, Germany, consulting.

I recommend reading the paper (see the preceding reference). The key takeaways are:

- There was no one-size-fits-all – they each used what worked for them.
- The journey took time and had setbacks along the way, which were taken as lessons not as reasons to assign blame.
- The companies embraced continuous change and didn't fight it.
- Companies that embraced technology adapted quicker.
- Continuous change and adaption was not a 'big bang' transformation.
- An experimental culture with a focus on proving in market was more effective than paper business cases.
- Ways of working were directly connected to business results – if your ways of working are not improving your business results, you need to change them.

Common characteristics across the research sites included:

- **Being customer-centric:** Focusing on added value and innovation rather than short-term profits.
- **Managers as enablers:** Managers seeing themselves as enablers who remove roadblocks, not controllers.
- **Putting people first:** Large focus on utilising the full talent and capacity of everyone. People were engaged and happy at work.
- **Ways of working:** Implementing autonomous teams and networks of teams, even at large scale. Iterative ways of working with a constant focus on customer. Transparency and continuous improvement on products, services and work methods.
- **Adaptability:** Listening and adapting to market changes rather than fixed plans.
- **Communication:** Being open and conversational, not controlled and bureaucratic.
- **Values:** Ensuring an egalitarian and collaboration friendly culture; safe to share your opinion.

WHAT CAN WE LEARN?

So, what can we learn from agility masters and the common characteristics of these organisations? Before I deep dive into some agility masters, I want to call your attention to two common problems:

- **No guarantees.** The other big takeaway is that agility is not a 'guarantee' for business results. Instead, it will help you adapt quicker to market changes to improve the likelihood of success. There are no guarantees of business success and no silver bullets.
- **A language problem.** I know a lot of people in organisations that are not succeeding at agile will look at the preceding list and state, 'Yes, we are doing all of these things, and yet we are still not successful.' The problem here is language. For example, people see the word 'autonomy' and think 'squads', and that they have squads so therefore they are autonomous.

Lost in translation examples

Autonomy

Having autonomous teams means that teams are E2E (end to end) cross-functional, responsible for taking an idea into market without any handoffs or dependencies on other teams. Most organisations today have set up teams to be 'autonomous', but each team still has handoffs for decisions, approvals and deployments, dependencies on other teams for another tech stack, and on and on it goes. This is not autonomy.

Iterative ways of working

It's quite common for organisations to take this to mean 'sprints' and 'quarterly increments', but what is actually happening is that an increment is just a block of work where nothing is delivered to a customer; it is just a segment in time. How much of your work is being put into the hands of a real customer?

Value

The definition of value is also misinterpreted. Frequently organisations consider a released feature and an unreleased feature to be the same as value. This thinking leads to 'feature factories', where organisations produce feature after feature but nothing positive happens from a business or a customer perspective. A better definition of value is 'a feature that is put into a real customer's hands and we have "proven" that the feature is adding value to the customer by tracking the user behaviour to ensure it is being used at the frequency expected'. So how much value does your organisation produce on a regular basis?

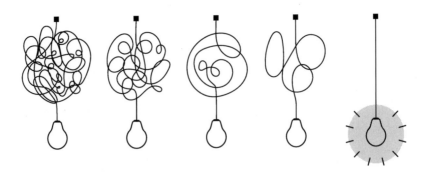

*

Before diving head on into your agility transformation, I recommend spending some time learning from agility masters so you can recognise what *real* agility looks like. This will save you a lot of time and pain down the track. Over the next few pages you will see there are some clear trailblazers in the art of agility.

MICROSOFT CORPORATION

Organisational history and context

Microsoft is a company I admire. It has completed many successful transformations and it continues to adapt and change and stay relevant.

Microsoft made its original successes with MS-DOS and was the first software company to reach $1B in revenue, capturing 90% of the PC market with Windows. Since then it has had many successes (Xbox, Office, Windows, Azure) and failures (phones, Edge, MSN). As a company, it is growing and transforming all the time, testing and learning with new products and acquisitions. It would have been easy for Microsoft to rest on its laurels and focus on their cash cow, but they didn't. They relentlessly adapted to changing market and consumer needs, sometimes creating trends, other times following.

In 2004, Microsoft was like any other successful big organisation: fat and bureaucratic.[8] They started their agile journey in 2008, and in 2015 it became a company-wide mandate.[9]

In 2014, Satya Nadella was made CEO and doubled down on innovation. His vision was to create an organisation with 70,000 innovators, rather than simply having a business unit for innovation.[10] He wished to unleash the power of every employee in the organisation, not just a select few with a growth focus. This became a company-wide initiative and encouraged everyone in the company to share their ideas with others, experiment and test and learn, rather than stating innovation was the responsibility of only one team or unit.

Business results (2017–22; five-year period)

- 254% share price uplift from US$74 to US$266.
- 200% revenue uplift from US$96B to US$198B.
- 300% net profit uplift from US$25B to US$73B.

Agility patterns of Microsoft[11]

- Mandated agile, but crafted their own. Did not use an off-the-shelf agile framework.
- Transition to agility started in 2008. It is an ongoing journey.
- CEO embraced it. It was company-wide and was top-down and bottom-up.
- Unleashed the power of everyone in the organisation rather than a select few at the top.
- Focused on their people and team and making them happy and valued.
- Ensured growth is continuous and ongoing rather than a big bang transformation.
- Experimented and had product successes and failures, and pivoted when needed.

Key takeaways

- **Agility can be done successfully in a large company.**
  An organisation can be agile regardless of its size. In fact, an adaptive operational model is the key to Microsoft's success. It enabled Microsoft to transform what value it offers its customers many times. With each failure and success, they adapted, they 'end of lifed' products and created new ones. They focused on the customer, not on the products.
- **Companies that are not agile to begin with can be agile at a later date.** On this journey, as Microsoft scaled and got successful they got bloated and slow. It happens to the best of companies. However, they changed; they put a focus on organisational fitness and introduced agility.
- **People-first culture.** They also put a focus on a people-first culture and leadership from the top.

So many people will say, you can't scale agility. This is simply not true. Of course you can. Microsoft is living proof.

GOOGLE (ALPHABET)

Organisational history and context

The Google web search engine was officially launched in 1998 and quickly diversified, with Google News in 2002, Gmail in 2004, Google Maps in 2005, Google Chrome in 2008 and Google+ in 2011. In 2005, Google was valued at nearly US$52B, making it one of the world's biggest media companies by stock market value.

Unlike Microsoft, Google embraced agility from its inception. However, it makes no declarations of being agile and does not use any off-the-shelf frameworks. Instead, this time similar to Microsoft, it has grown its own fit-for-purpose way of working, with a heavy focus on autonomy, innovation and allowing people and teams to experiment and solve their own problems. Google has made many declarations about being an employee-first, data-driven company, and passionately believes in identifying and role modelling good behaviours that deliver excellence.

People first and evidence-based are part of Google's DNA

· **Project Aristotle** was a study into what makes a team effective at Google – a tribute to Aristotle's quote, 'the whole is greater than the sum of its parts' (as the Google researchers believed employees can do more together than working alone).[12]

The biggest finding was that it mattered less who was on a team and it mattered more how the team interacted. They ranked what made a team successful (in order of importance):

- *Psychological safety:* People felt safe to share an opinion, make a mistake and not be judged or blamed.
- *Dependability:* Everyone played an active role and they were mutually accountable for an outcome.
- *Structure and clarity:* Everyone understood the role they needed to play and what they were trying to achieve.

- *Meaning:* They gained a sense of purpose from their work, which could be personal.
- *Impact:* They felt their work was having a real impact for a customer or the organisation.

- **Project Oxygen** was a Google study into what makes a great manager. This is a great study, because initially the researchers tried to prove that managers were not important and were not required at Google, but this was not the finding of the research. It showed that people thrived with a good manager; the problem wasn't managers, but bad managers. They found a good manager:[13]

  - is a good coach
  - empowers teams and does not micromanage
  - creates an inclusive team environment, showing concern for success and wellbeing
  - is productive and results oriented
  - is a good communicator (listens and shares information)
  - supports career development and discusses performance
  - has a clear vision or strategy for the team
  - has relevant skillsets and capability to advise the team
  - collaborates across the entire company
  - is a strong decision maker.

Business results (2017–22; five-year period)

- 252% share price uplift from US$48 to US$121.
- 252% revenue uplift from US$110B to US$278B.
- >500% net profit uplift from US$13B to US$72B.

Agility patterns of Google

- Mandated agile, but crafted their own; did not use an off-the-shelf agile framework.
- Embraced agility from day one.
- Used evidence-based approach not opinion-led.
- Unleashed the power of everyone in the organisation rather than a select few at the top.

- Focused on their people and team and making them happy and valued.
- Ensured growth is continuous and ongoing rather than a big bang transformation.
- Experimented and had product successes and failures, and pivoted when needed.

Key takeaways

- **Agile from the start because they had no preconceived concepts of how a company should work.** Google's journey has been very different to Microsoft's. They embraced a new adaptive operational model from the start. As a young start-up, old bureaucratic ways of working were not a concept they had experienced, so they were open to doing what worked for them with no old-style rules and boundaries on how a company must operate for success.
- **Evidenced approach to outcomes.** The next point of difference of Google is that they 'seek to understand' with their research projects, and put a heavy focus on facts, not on opinions of executives.
- **Experimentation and innovation culture.** Google also experienced a lot of successes and failures and, similar to Microsoft, they learnt from the failures and pivoted when necessary, using evidenced-based metrics to make decisions.

7-ELEVEN JAPAN[14]

Organisational history and context

7-Eleven was brought to Japan in 1973 by Masatoshi Ito and his company Ito-Yokado. In 1991, Ito-Yokado took a majority stake in 7-Eleven's US owner Southland, fully acquiring it in 2005 and establishing Seven & i Holdings as part of a corporate restructure. There are at the time of writing approximately 20,000 7-Eleven stores in Japan, and more stores in Japan than in the United States.

Key organisational highlights[15]

- Highly evolved technology-led business strategy.
- Innovation and business growth is at the core – 70% of all products sold each year are new.

- Each store makes local decisions based on centrally designed systems and processes.
- All organisational information is digitised.
- There are 70,000 nodes linking stores, head offices, suppliers and distribution centres.
- Digitised processes allow stores to order and receive food three times a day.
- Emphasis on training and mentoring all employees. Counsellors visit stores twice a week.
- Gross margins per store have increased from 5% to 30% over eight-year period.
- Stock turnover has decreased from 25.5 to 9 days.

Business results

- Revenue ¥850B in 2020, up nearly 30% in eight years.
- Profit ¥230B in 2022, up 30% YoY.[16]

Agility patterns of 7-Eleven Japan

- Utilised lean and agile tactics – very focused on evidence-based decisions and digitally enabled.
- Loosely coupled stores but highly aligned and integrated with local decision-making for speed.
- Focused on flow, reducing bottlenecks.
- Utilised multi-cross-functional teams with a smart, measurable objective to align everyone.

Key takeaways

- **Evidence.** Evidence-based innovation with fact-based decisions on what products to sell.
- **Digital first.** Digitally enabled organisation run on data not opinions for fast decision-making.
- **Continuous learning and mastery.** Focus on training staff to ensure quality uplifts.
- **Agility and lean operating model directly tied to the bottom line.** Clear WHY on approach.

BOSCH POWER TOOLS

Organisational history and context

Bosch was founded over 100 years ago in Germany and is a massive organisation, employing over 400,000 people, with Bosch Power Tools making up approximately 20,000 people. They started a transformation journey in approximately 2016 as things had started to sour. Business growth was declining and they were struggling to adapt quickly to market changes associated with globalisation, digitisation and the fact that their customer had changed from retailer to end user.

Their transformation approach started with three key questions (their WHY):

- Are we close enough to our users?
- Are we innovative enough?
- Are we fast and flexible enough?

They wanted to move to an agile-based approach for their organisation, but rejected commercial off-the-shelf agile products and instead came up with their own grassroots agility ways of working. They developed five key principles:

- Strong purpose.
- Permanent cross-functional teams.
- Flat hierarchies.
- New understanding of leadership.
- Open communication.

Effectively, they transitioned from one big company into nine different, smaller autonomous companies, each with their own P&L. Each business unit was allowed to decide how best to apply these principles – that is, units had autonomy to decide what worked for them.

Business results[17]

- €5.8B in 2021.
- 16% uplift (YoY revenue from 2020 to 2021).
- Pivoted to focus on business growth in batteries and cordless appliances.

Agility patterns at Bosch Power Tools

- Implemented transformation team, made up of volunteers from each unit.
- Ensured autonomy, through splitting the organisation into nine smaller units.
- Didn't spend excessive time producing a plan; started with action quickly.
- Experimented, learnt fast, started small.
- Shared ideas on what worked in each unit, so they could learn.

Key takeaways

- **Move from silos to E2E cross-functional units.** Bosch did a lot of soul searching on what operating model would work and how they could introduce speed. They turned their oil tanker into multiple speedboats successfully. This change took time, with obstacles along the way.
- **Pull not push model.** Each speedboat moved and changed at its own pace. There was no one-size-fits-all. They experimented with new ways of working in small pockets. They had control over what they tried and what they didn't try. When something worked, they shared the idea with the broader community and why it worked, using evidence. Other units could choose to try what was presented, but they were not forced to. This allowed people to control their own journey to mastery. They could 'pull' other ideas in if they wanted, and these methods were not pushed onto business units.

LINKEDIN

Organisational history and context

Launched in 2003, in August 2004 LinkedIn reached 1 million users. In March 2006, LinkedIn achieved its first month of profitability. In April 2007, LinkedIn reached 10 million users. In February 2008, LinkedIn launched a mobile version of the site. Its IPO was in 2011 for US$45 a share, which was the same year they transitioned to CEO-endorsed agile ways of working. Again, they designed something that was fit for purpose for themselves. They did not buy a commercial agile framework off the shelf, but used many practices that worked for them (scrum, XP, devops, continuous development, trunk-based development). In 2016, they were acquired by Microsoft for US$196 a share.

Business results (2017–21; five-year period)

- \>400% revenue uplift from US$2.271B to US$10.289B.
- 65% individual users uplift from 491M to 756M.
- \>300% enterprise accounts uplift 18M to 57M.

Agility patterns at LinkedIn

- Adopted enterprise-wide in 2011, set by the CEO, and they stopped development for two months to get ready.[18]
- Used multiple fit-for-purpose agility tactics that were right for them.
- Ensured technology-led; business and technology tightly aligned as one, but with a focus on autonomy.
- Enforced speed to market as a key feature, moving from monthly feature releases to twice daily.
- Implemented continuous deployment to reduce risk and increase speed to market.

Key takeaways

- **Customer first.** As a regular user of LinkedIn, I have watched their journey for a long time. I am impressed with their ability to keep their users engaged, and how they have transformed from résumés to jobs to content to learning. LinkedIn is probably one of the only social media platforms where I have increased my usage over the years rather than decreased my usage. It has managed to keep me engaged, which is hard for any organisation to do over time, especially a social platform.
- **Top-down.** LinkedIn had a CEO-driven agility transformation, and he made the bold decision to stop all business change for two months. I am surprised by the boldness! This is a CEO who meant business and was going all-in to change his organisation for success. I admire a CEO who is willing to take this risk.

ERICSSON[19]

Organisational history and context

Ericsson is over 140 years old. It is a Swedish multinational networking and telecommunications company. The company sells infrastructure and services for telecommunications service providers, including 3G, 4G and 5G equipment, and IP and optical transport systems. Ericsson has been a major contributor to the development of the telecommunications industry, and is one of the leaders in 5G. It employs approximately 100,000 people globally.

Business results (2017–21; four-year period)

- Approximately 250% share price uplift from 46SEK to 116SEK.
- 15% revenue uplift from US$23.6B to US$27B.
- Net profit uplift from US$–4.4B to US$2.646B.

Agility patterns of Ericsson[20]

- Started in 2014 and started small. Put a large focus on lean, flow and value.
- Tied business drivers of time to market, quality and return on investment to approach.
- Ensured rollout was incremental. No area was forced. Encouraged an 'opt-in model'.
- Endured setbacks along the way – fully cross-functional didn't work for them.
- Measured success as a critical factor in deciding if it was working or not.
- Realised changing culture and mindset were critical to allowing change to stick.
- Provided flexibility to teams on estimation from single point to ranges, which gave safety to teams.

Key takeaways

- **Start small, don't rush it.** There was no big bang transformation. It was small, incremental improvements.

- **Pull not push model.** You can read a lot into an organisation that does not force change on teams. It is a confident stance that people will embrace the change, if it is good enough and they are ready for it.
- **Evidenced based.** Success was achieving by moving away from opinions. This allowed them to get greater chances of success.

CH ROBINSON

Organisational history and context

CH Robinson was founded in 1905 and now has almost 20,000 employees. It is a multimodal transportation services and 3PL (third-party logistics) business. It is currently the largest 3PL in the United States. The company offers freight, transportation, transportation management, brokerage and warehousing. This includes air, road and ocean freight.

Business results (2017–22; five-year period)

- >50% share price uplift from US$76 to US$117.
- >40% revenue uplift from US$14.869B to US$21.231B.
- >65% net profit uplift from US$505M to US$844M.

Agility patterns of CH Robinson

- Realised bureaucracy and age of the organisation was making CH Robinson slow and inefficient.
- Started exploring agility in 2011. Progress was slow at first.
- Initially focused on going through the motions, processes, tools, ceremonies, iterating.
- Joined the Learning Consortium in 2015, uplifted their agility program.
- Started to rebuild teams without dependencies, a tough feat with old legacy systems.
- Introduced cross-functional E2E teams.
- Put a focus on speed to market, going from releasing quarterly to daily.
- Ensured agility was organisation-wide and the focus was on customers and meeting their needs.

Key takeaways

- **They failed upfront with common mistakes.** CH Robinson made all the basic mistakes on their first try. Then they paused, they reflected, they joined the Learning Consortium and they created an open community where each organisation learnt from the others. And then they brought back some targeted changes after spending some time understanding what agility was.
- **Speed to value was king.** They decided to put a key focus on speed to value as their productivity measure. This allowed them to get targeted on where to focus for success.

BARCLAYS BANK

Organisational history and context

Barclays' history dates back to before 1700 and it now has over 85,000 employees. Barclays has a rich history of innovation and adaptation, introducing the first cash machine in 1967 and the first debit card in 1987. Barclays is proudly digitally led in its strategy and always willing to experiment so that it stays competitive. Barclays is the second-ranked bank in the UK and plays in the global market also.

Business results (2017–22; five-year period)

- Share price drop from £179 (2017) to £145 (2021).
- Revenue uplift from £21.076B (2017) to £21.94B (2021).
- Net profit uplift from £1.301B (2017) to £7.266B (2021).

Agility patterns of Barclays[21]

- Started their journey under Jonathan Smart in 2015.[22]
- Ensured not just technology – business *and* technology.
- Implemented over scale – one of the world's largest agile implementations.
- Used multiple approaches, not one-size-fits-all (disciplined agile, devops, lean, agile).
- Focused on throughput, better collaboration and removing impediments.
- Introduced the concept of four levels of teams for agility maturity.

- Focused on business outcomes not agile frameworks and experimentation.

Key takeaways

The key takeaway here is that you should read Jonathan Smart's book *Sooner Safer Happier*. He talks through in detail how he transformed a large organisation with agility. I admire and respect this book – I can tell from reading it that Jonathan is a hands-on practitioner who has lived through this change and transformation journey.

BMW

Organisational history and context

BMW was founded in 1916, originally by an aircraft producer to produce aircraft engines. It wasn't until 1928 that BMW moved into automotive production. It is now one of the world's leading premium manufacturers of automobiles and motorcycles, with just under 120,000 employees globally. BMW has shown an ability to focus on growth and innovation with a move from engines to cars to motorcycles to other mobility devices, and now a focus on electric cars

Business results

- Revenue uplift from US$104B (2016) to US$131B (2021).
- Net profit uplift from US$7.595B (2016) to US$14.649B (2021).

Agility patterns of BMW[23]

- Started their agility journey in 2016.
- Used multiple approaches, not one-size-fits-all (lean, BizDevOps, value streams, products, LeSS, SAFe).
- Introduced portfolios with minimal governance and focus on autonomy not policing.
- Changed funding model to support products and value and move away from business cases.
- Ensured digital-enabled business strategy.
- Implemented top-down and bottom-up approach – enterprise-wide focus.

- Didn't focus on the how; focused on the outcome.
- Created benefits that include:
  - 200% uplift in release frequency from 12 to 24 a year
  - significant reduction in defects and time to resolve defects.

Key takeaways

- **Focus on why not how.** A heavy focus was put on outcomes not frameworks, and outcome delivery was measured.
- **Reduced governance and changed funding model.** Frequently governance and funding are blockers, not enablers. People who perform these roles feel it is their responsibility to 'police' others. I love that a large organisation such as BMW recognised these things needed to change for speed and that there were multiple models for governance and funding, and that their current model did not reduce risk any more than the new model.
- **Evidence-based decisions.** These led to significant reductions in time to market and cost (new feature releases from every four months to every three weeks).

SPOTIFY

Organisational history and context

It would be remiss of me to not include Spotify in this list because so many organisations 'copy' the Spotify agile model, with 'tribes' and 'chapters'. I include Spotify for this reason alone. Spotify, while uplifting its revenue and subscribers, has never been profitable and it would not meet my definition of agility mastery, but it is referenced so frequently in relation to agile I felt it important to include. Spotify is famous in the agile world quite simply due to some cute little videos and the power of marketing[24], though they are good and I recommend checking them out.

Spotify was founded in 2006 and is an Swedish audio and media content streaming service with approximately 7000 employees. It is one of the world's largest music streaming services with approximately 433M active monthly users and 188M paying subscribers. It floated on the NYSE in 2018.

Business results (2018–22; five-year period)

- Negative – share price drop from US$113 (Dec. 2018) to US$78 (Dec. 2022).
- 300% revenue uplift from €2.94B to €9B.
- Negative net profit – most interestingly, Spotify does not make profit.

Agility patterns of Spotify[25, 26]

- Ensured people and culture first.
- Promoted team autonomy.
- Implemented technology organisation with a service-led architecture (suited to autonomy).
- Encouraged innovation – 10% of time dedicated to it.

Key takeaways[27]

The key takeaway is that Spotify never claimed to follow the Spotify model! The model was a cute promotional video that focused on storytelling rather than reality. Welcome to marketing and branding – these videos were taken as fact and organisations spent tens of millions replicating the model. I recommend watching the videos because they are cute and fun.[*]

The key takeaway is simple: none of it was real.

US FEDERAL GOVERNMENT[28]

Organisational history and context

I have included the US Federal Government because I felt it was important to show how diverse the take up of agile is and why organisations move to it. The Federal Government have surprisingly written quite a lot about this topic. Their message was that they spend US$90B a year on technology and they were tired of the old way of working, with frequent cost overruns, schedule slippages and not achieving business goals, so they said it was simply time to embrace doing things differently.

---

[*] www.youtube.com/watch?v=4GK1NDTWbkY.

Agility patterns of the Federal Government

- Implemented cultural change – moved away from top-down hierarchy to self-managing teams.
- Increased collaboration and reduced silos.
- Promoted multiple lean and devops methods.
- Ensured data and metrics driven to measuring success.
- Moved vendor landscape away from fixed price and scope to flexible contracts.
- Took greater accountability for outsourcing success.
- Reduced governance bureaucracy by recognising that it did not stop failures.
- Used timeboxing as a tactic for estimation and scheduling.

Key takeaways

- **If they can, you can!** The US Federal Government should be an inspiration for everyone. If they can change their operational model with all the complexities of their world, anyone can do it!

- **Timeboxing – when will it be finished?** I will call out this tactic because it is a favourite of mine. Senior executives always want to know when something will be finished. To be honest, I do too! But I understand how hard it is to answer this question. If a team have not done something before, how can they know how long it will take to complete? This is especially the case when they don't have any visibility of what else might come their way. So, the best way to get an accurate estimate is with timeboxing. Timeboxing is when you present time as the number one requirement to the team. You tell them you need something finished by XX date and then they work backwards on the work to be done. You help them prioritise their work and you accept that the items at the bottom of the list probably won't get done. I have an extremely high accuracy rating with timeboxing for getting something delivered on time.

*

Agility masters observe and don't copy. I have taken you through these agility masters so you can understand that there are many ways to achieve agility and see how other organisations have achieved success, and to do some myth-busting such as you cannot do agile at scale – of course you can! It is important to learn to recognise what agile looks like, so you can learn when you are on the wrong path and you can course correct.

WILL AGILITY GUARANTEE SUCCESS?

The short answer is *maybe*. There are no guarantees to business success and no silver bullets. If someone promises this, leave the room immediately.

However …

Agility, **if done properly**, yes, agility will give you a greater likelihood of business success.

SO, REMIND ME – WHAT DID THE AGILITY MASTERS DO DIFFERENTLY?

- **Focus on customers not products:** They put customer value at the heart of everything they do.
- **Evidence-based decisions:** They brought scientific methods to running their business.
- **Small bets not big bets:** Agile encourages test and learn and small releases not big releases, so you can validate assumptions in market *before* you spend all your budget on an idea that will not work.
- **Ability to pivot in market:** Small releases mean it is cheaper and quicker to adapt to changing market conditions without big overheads.
- **Incremental roll out:** Agile encourages teams to put features that they think will add value into customers' hands quickly and cheaply, and then validate by monitoring customer usage to see if the features do add value. If a feature does not add value, it is not enhanced or is dropped.

- **Speed of decisioning:** Putting a focus on everyone in the organisation via networked teams rather than a bureaucratic hierarchy with a small number of leaders at the top to make all the decisions means that decision-making is quick and given to those closest to the work.
- **Speed and continuous improvement:** Putting a focus on outcomes not outputs means it's cheaper to deliver quality products to customers that meet their needs.
- **People focus:** People-led cultural transformation is focused on meeting people's needs instead of ignoring them.
- **Continuous learning:** The mantra of act, measure, adapt and continuously change is an agile mindset. This means that learning is built into the DNA of the organisation so teams feel appreciated and have a sense of purpose, while being given new skills and learning to keep them relevant, which increases confidence and motivation.

So agility really is a no-brainer – again, I must stress, *if done properly.*

OKAY, ARE YOU GOING TO SHOW ME HOW TO ACHIEVE SOME OF THESE THINGS?

Yes, I will walk you through targeted tactics you can try to achieve the aspects just outlined. However, it is too early to move to HOW. We need to focus first on WHAT and WHY. The next section of the book is focused on what agility is, how you will know if you have achieved it, and what the most common pitfalls are that you should try to avoid.

CHAPTER 3

WHAT IS AGILE AND HOW WILL YOU KNOW IF YOU HAVE ACHIEVED IT?

'WE CANNOT BECOME WHAT
WE WANT TO BE BY REMAINING
WHERE WE ARE.'

MAX DE PREE

IS YOUR ORGANISATION AGILE?

Such a simple question.

It's not as simple as it sounds to answer, unfortunately. The word 'agile' has lost all meaning. There is a lot of emperor's new clothing. As a consequence, I have dedicated a section of the book to helping you assess if you are agile. If you want to have a fast and adaptive organisation, it is important to know what one looks like.

I have two methods for this:

· **Agility pulse check:** A short, quick assessment, exactly like taking your own pulse.
· **Agility fitness test:** A more comprehensive test, like a physical fitness test.

AGILITY PULSE CHECK

Here is a simple 10-point checklist; does your organisation fit this definition? Are you doing all these things?

1. **Customer and business value:** Value is in the hands of your customers and you have evidence that they like it and are using it, and you focus on proving upfront that your paper assumptions will deliver the required value before spending all your budget. The best way to think of customer value is 'value consumed'.

   Business value is that you have made a profit.

   You are focused externally on market and customer conditions and not internally.

2. **Clarity:** The people in your organisation have clarity on what is and isn't important and everyone is aligned.

3. **Speed to market:** Time to value is measured and baselined, and value is released frequently to customers (at least quarterly). Wastage on the customer value delivery chain is quantified with continuous improvement to reduce impact.

4. **People-centric:** You have evidence that your team and customers are happy and psychological safety is high.

5. **Governance:** The system of 'getting work done' is transparent and observable, and executives and teams use the same data. All decisions are based on evidence not opinion. Governance is enabling, with a focus on not blocking and policing teams.

6. **Risk:** Everything is delivered in small batches of value, so that priorities can change and you have the ability to pivot and adapt with minimal impact.

7. **Quality:** Quality is quantified and traced against change to see if it's improving or declining.

8. **Team structures and organisation design:** People are working cross-functionally not in silos, and have a common customer and business goal. Teams are flexible and adaptive and can change easily without a restructure. Organisation structure is more like an ecosystem than a hierarchy. Flexibility and adaptability are built in.

9. **Business growth and innovation:** Is your organisation static or growing? How do you know? How much effort are you dedicating to new business models and growth opportunities?

10. **Learning and adapting:** Are your teams continuously improving and getting better at what they do? How do you know? Your teams need to be showing tangible uplift in how they perform their roles, and you need to be supporting and enabling this journey for them. Your people are your most expensive organisational asset; treat them wisely.

*

So how does your organisation rate – are you an agile-based organisation? Most organisations will not rate too well to begin with – that's okay. Becoming fast and adaptive and changing to new ways of working will take time.

AGILITY FITNESS TEST

Now it's time to get serious about your organisational fitness and agility. Remember:

- Getting fit is hard.
- Getting strong is hard.
- Maintaining the fitness is hard.

That is why so many people aren't fit and strong. If you are looking for a shortcut, you will never be fit.

It is important to assess your agility fitness on a regular basis; doing so will create alignment on what you should focus on to get the greatest bang for your buck. It will make the problems visible and create a common discussion for everyone to get behind, using evidence rather than opinions.

There are 10 different levers to assessing your organisational health and agility fitness. They should be assessed on a regular basis – I recommend quarterly, with baselines.

This fitness test assesses the same criteria as the pulse check, but is a more comprehensive test designed to help you become targeted on your path forward. It will help you pinpoint areas of improvement in your current fitness. This will enable targeted solutions to solve your problems.

Before starting any difficult journey, and frequently during that difficult journey, assessment is required. Think of it like a GPS – it will help point you in the right direction. This will prepare you for your journey ahead and help you decide what areas you need to focus on.

Remember, to get the best outcome, incorporate the following approach:

- Gather evidence, not opinions.
- Ensure the evidence represents the full picture, not a small skewed picture.
- Remember observation is a powerful method for evidence collection.
- Keep in mind trends are important, with frequent measuring required.

So let's dive more deeply into the 10 criteria in this agility fitness test. Does your business meet the following criteria? Answer yes or no to the following questions to establish the current level of agility in your organisation.

1. Customer and business value (working on the right things)

- **Categorisation:** Value is categorised into two types: business and customer.   Y   N
- **Value:** Is measured with in-market usage and frequency of release.   Y   N
- **Evidence:** Value is tracked and trended.   Y   N
- **Fast feedback loops:** In-market behaviour is used to prioritise work.   Y   N
- **ROI:** The cost of producing the value is related to the value released.   Y   N
- **CSAT:** Customer **SAT**isfaction score and feedback are collected and aligned with value consumed.   Y   N

2. Clarity

- **Cross-functionality:** Objectives are cross-functional not functional.   Y   N
- **Clarity:** There is one list of priorities for the organisation that is ranked clearly.   Y   N
- **Less is more:** Priority is a small number of things, not a large number of things.   Y   N
- **No hidden work:** Planning covers everything that a team is working on, not a subset of work.   Y   N
- **Work in progress:** Each team limits WIP with a focus on finishing before starting.   Y   N
- **Effort:** There is a visible correlation between effort and priority.   Y   N
- **Alignment:** Who is assigned to each priority is clear and obvious.   Y   N
- **Goals:** SMART goals are in place to describe each priority and benefit to be realised.   Y   N
- **Prove don't assume:** Organisation proves a concept with a small bet before making a big bet.   Y   N

3. Speed to market

- **Flow:** You know how long it takes to get an idea into market.   Y   N

- **Lead:** You know how long it takes to get an idea ready to build.   Y   N
- **Cycle:** You know how long it takes to get an idea built and into market.   Y   N
- **Deployment frequency:** You know the frequency of deployments.   Y   N
- **Trends:** Speed to market is tracked and trended across all teams.   Y   N
- **Evidence-based:** Tracking is evidence-based not opinion-based.   Y   N
- **Waste:** Bottlenecks impacting speed are visible and time impacts are known.   Y   N
- **Categorised:** Bottlenecks are categorised into lead or cycle bottlenecks to show problems.   Y   N
- **Optimising:** Speed to market is reducing year on year.   Y   N
- **Consistency:** All teams use the same definitions to ensure accuracy.   Y   N
- **Shared learning:** Teams share their challenges and discuss solutions together.   Y   N
- **Deadlines:** Are not given to the team or imposed by people not doing the work.   Y   N

4. People-centric (happy people)

- **Inclusive:** Definitions include all employment types and partners.   Y   N
- **eSAT:** Employee **SAT**isfaction is tracked.   Y   N
- **Optimising:** Action is taken to improve eSAT.   Y   N
- **Psychological safety:** People feel safe to share their opinions without retribution.   Y   N
- **Healthy conflict:** People are given the skills and opportunity to have healthy conflict.   Y   N
- **Mastery:** People feel their skills are improving and you are invested in their career.   Y   N
- **Purpose:** People know what their role is and how it delivers on purpose.   Y   N
- **Restructures:** Are not a means of reducing cost.   Y   N

5. Governance

- **Organisational health:** Visible and transparent and based on evidence not opinions.   Y   N
- **Single source:** Teams and executives use the same data.   Y   N
- **Decisions with minimal information:** Teams are not expected to have all the answers upfront (value, costs, funding are incremental).   Y   N

6. Risk (small batches of work)

- **Small not big bets:** Paper assumptions are not funded; concepts should be proven.   Y   N
- **Experimentation:** Is encouraged so that teams can learn quickly what will deliver.   Y   N
- **Small not big:** Objectives and work to be done are parcelled into small batches.   Y   N
- **Value realised:** A batch of work must have value realised for it to be completed.   Y   N
- **Risk:** Is reduced using small batches of work.   Y   N
- **Ability to pivot:** Small batches are set up so that if a priority changes it has minimal impact.   Y   N

7. Quality

- **Change failure rate:** Every change is tracked for its relationship to failure.   Y   N
- **Mean time to recover:** How long it takes a problem to be resolved is known.   Y   N
- **Trends:** Quality is trended every month to see if it is improving or declining.   Y   N
- **Customer impact:** Is visible for each failure.   Y   N

8. Team structures and organisation design

- **Objectives:** There is a direct relationship between objective and definition of team.   Y   N

- **Cross-functional not silos:** A team is a cross-functional group of people who work together to achieve an objective.   Y N
- **Prioritisation:** Cross-functional teams have one set of priorities.   Y N
- **Minimal dependencies:** Take into consideration constraints or dependencies like tech stack boundaries to reduce handoffs and complexity of completing work.   Y N
- **Team handoffs:** Team is rarely impacted by another team to complete their work.   Y N
- **Flexibility and adaptability:** Definition of team is fluid depending on need and priority.   Y N
- **Autonomy:** Teams have autonomy to decide how they achieve the work.   Y N
- **Alignment:** Teams do not decide on the what, they align to organisational goals and focus.   Y N
- **Collaboration:** Is more important than documentation.   Y N

9. Business growth and innovation

- **Team performance:** Teams monitor their own performance and results are transparent.   Y N
- **Speed of decisioning:** Does not impact delivery of value with teams.   Y N
- **Alignment:** Between people, work, metrics and funding is visible and well understood.   Y N
- **Diversification:** The business spends a portion of its funding on growth initiatives.   Y N

10. Learning and adapting

- **Predictability:** Is tracked for learning – what did we say we would do? What did we do?   Y N
- **Core business:** Core business is known and well understood.   Y N
- **Innovation/high failure:** Is welcomed to encourage innovation.   Y N

IMPLEMENTING THE AGILITY TEST

When I help an organisation custom design their agility journey, I use this fitness test as a starting point to establish possible paths forward. There are two ways to use the test.

Interviews

Spend time interviewing a range of people across multiple teams in your organisation, including the CEO and all executive leaders. I always include people from different layers of the organisation so I can validate if messages at the top are consistent with messages at the bottom.

An interview approach is a reasonably quick way to assess fitness; however, it is not foolproof because it is reliant on people's opinions and their perception of the current situation. I frequently will recommend the interview-style fitness test as a good way to start the journey; it will feel safer to your people and is a softer way to approach assessment upfront.

Observation

Like all scientific approaches, an evidence-based approach is the gold standard. The way to achieve this in your organisation is to observe your teams and people in action rather than ask their opinions. This will give you a more accurate assessment of your organisation's health and performance. It takes longer, but it will get you to the heart of the matter more quickly. Organisations with high psychological safety are comfortable with this approach because they frequently welcome feedback and have already built this muscle.

*

Both approaches are effective. Like everything in life, it depends on the context of your organisation. Like all fitness tests, they only add value when you use them as a baseline and track your performance against key metrics on a regular basis. The intent is to prove your success. Anyone who is worth their salt will welcome such a journey.

CUSTOM DESIGNING YOUR AGILITY JOURNEY

The agility fitness test can be used throughout the rest of the book to help you decide where you should focus first. Remember that agility is not one thing, it is many things.

I have separated agility into three 'organisational muscle groups' to help you build your organisational fitness. Each group comes with its own workout series designed to strengthen that group.

Organisational muscle group	Workout series
Outcomes – first, fast and frequent	**I** – Inspire with a north star **M** – Measure what matters **P** – Prove don't assume **A** – Accelerate time to value **C** – Cadence, fast and frequent **T** – Transparency
Behaviours – behavioural-led cultural change	**F** – Make feedback normal **A** – Accountability with radical candour **C** – Healthy conflict management **E** – Energy multipliers and drainers **S** – Self-awareness
Organisational Mastery – building a continuous learning organisation	**L1** – Role model – observation **L2** – Learn by doing – assisted **L3** – Learn by doing – unassisted **L4** – Role model for others

Mapping your fitness assessment results to the muscle groups and workouts

Combine your fitness test results with the muscle groups and workouts to custom design your path forward and decide where to focus your time and energy.

Lots of 'no's in …	Focus on this muscle group	Use this workout
1. Customers and business value	Outcomes	I – Inspire with north star
2. Clarity	Outcomes	I – Inspire with north star
3. Speed to market	Outcomes	A – Accelerate time to value
4. People-centric	Behaviours	FACES
5. Governance	Outcomes	T – Transparency
6. Risk	Outcomes	A – Accelerate time to value
7. Quality	Outcomes	M – Measure what matters
8. Team structures and organisation design	Outcomes	A – Accelerate time to value
9. Business growth and innovation	Outcomes	P – Prove don't assume
10. Learning and adapting	Organisational mastery	Four levels of mastery

COMMON AGILE IMPLEMENTATION PITFALLS

As mentioned previously, initial attempts at making organisations agile frequently fail. This section of the book will help you understand where these organisations go wrong, so you can learn to recognise when you are on the right path and when you are not.

Most important is to not start your agility journey with HOW – start the journey with WHY. This journey is no different to any other journey. It will work better with WHY.

The most common approaches to rolling out agile in large organisations today are:

· Renaming teams to agile team names with new role types.
· Using a mandated framework that is very prescriptive, so that teams get lost following it.
· Moving to OKRs (objectives and key results) because 'everyone is doing them'.
· Implementing the big bang – finishing the old way of working on a Friday, starting the new way of working the next Monday.
· Designing upfront – all thinking is implemented without validating ideas.
· Focusing on HOW, not WHY or WHAT.
· Over-indexing on autonomy, with lots of mini teams, all creating their own backlog.
· Using work queues that become blocked or overflowing because everyone is putting work into other people's queues before filling their own work queue.
· Creating gridlock because the team and organisation structure are designed by HR, who only look at the people lens of team structure. Frequently teams are not being designed for workflow or minimising dependencies.

If any of these sound like your organisation – this is a warning bell.

MANAGING THE CHANGE PROCESS

Change fatigue

It is very common for people working in organisations to be feeling change fatigue from big-bang transformations. And they usually start or end with people losing their jobs, so they are not fun. Organisations need to move away from the word 'transformation' and lean into continuous but controlled change. More like a flywheel than a big bang. After all, agility is about small changes not big changes.

Too much change

Frequently, change is chaotic because organisations have multiple teams introducing different change initiatives. Change needs to be controlled. What change should a team go through for the month? It needs to come through a front door so you can assess the impact. Measure it up front. Agree on the capacity the team should dedicate to it. Cap it. Do not let continuous improvement get in the way of work. It should be helping the teams, not draining them.

Flywheel not big bang

The 'flywheel effect' is a concept developed in one of my favourite books, *Good to Great*. Good-to-great transformations never happen in one fell swoop. In building a great company or social sector enterprise, there is no single defining action, no grand program, no one killer innovation, no solitary lucky break, no miracle moment. Rather, the process resembles relentlessly pushing a giant, heavy flywheel, turn upon turn, building momentum until a point of breakthrough, and beyond. This enables people to embrace the change at a speed that works, so they can learn and adapt. When there are enough people on board, it will eventually build momentum and take on a life of its own, organisation-wide.

THE STARTING LINE

So far we have covered:

- common sentiments about agile and why they exist
- agile history and origins
- common implementation mistakes
- agility mastery – who has achieved it and how
- how to recognise agility
- the agility pulse check and fitness test.

Each of these is critical for starting your agility journey and shouldn't be rushed. Not understanding this context is where people and organisations go wrong, because they want to rush into HOW to do agility.

The agility fitness test you have completed will help you get the most of out of the rest of the book. It will help you assess which sections of the book will add most value to your organisation. If you use targeted agility tactics, you will have the ability to deliver some quick wins in your organisation. All the HOW tactics will focus on evidence so you can ensure you are actually uplifting your organisation with confidence.

All in all, this is a good starting position for custom designing your agility journey. However, before you get started, you need to find your WHY. *Why* do you want to become fast and adaptive? What do you think will happen if you achieve it?

CHAPTER 4
PUTTING THE <u>WHY</u> INTO YOUR JOURNEY

'START WITH WHY.'
SIMON SINEK

EVERY JOURNEY MUST START WITH WHY

Every journey must start with WHY. You need to have a reason for starting the journey. Your agility journey is no different. If you don't have a reason, it is hard to stay focused and on track. Your WHY is like the GPS. A journey to transforming your organisation into fast and adaptive is long and arduous, and at times you will feel like giving up, so a WHY is essential. When the going gets tough, it will help you to keep going and to feel like it is all worthwhile.

Ignite the spark

Your WHY can give you the excitement to take the journey and succeed at it, rather than merely doing it because you could. You must light the spark for everyone who needs to go on the journey, and that spark must be personalised and relevant for them or it won't resonate. You will not light a spark for everyone if you show them a framework and tell them they need to use it. People do not like it when they have a new way of working forced upon them by people who don't fully understand what they do – can you blame them? Allow people to contribute to their own journey. They are more likely to accept it than when others are deciding for them.

Don't be reactive

One of the main reasons organisations start an agility journey is that they are losing out in the market and competitors are releasing value to customers earlier or they are disrupting. Unfortunately, this is a reactive reason; catching this problem proactively before it happens is the win. Fit and strong organisations don't rest on their laurels when they are doing well. They know things change fast, and maintaining fitness becomes the name of the game.

Make it relevant

I have seen so many agility journeys over the years that are not relevant to the people or the work being performed. The slide decks are glossy, the messages look great, and if you read it everything seems logical – the problem is it isn't real. No one knows how to go from glossy pack to reality. The change is in the hands of people with no experience or skills. These are journeys created without a WHY that resonates. If your organisation is extremely large, it is really hard to have one WHY journey for everyone. I recommend creating multiple WHYs; this is agility after all. Break the WHY down! So that it still resonates. WHY must be close to the customer and the people and the work to make it real. Be creative in how you get to your WHY. Agility is not the goal – it's a critical business enabler.

AGILITY IS A CRITICAL BUSINESS ENABLER

Business growth is a great WHY

So, what is your WHY? How will you decide? Agility is frequently closely tied to enabling business growth and helping organisations evolve, accelerate and scale so that they can outperform their competitors. If your agile program is not helping you with this, you need to course correct and do things differently. Your agility program should be tied to real, tangible business objectives. If it is not helping you win in the market or has not delivered proven business results, change it! Stop accepting second-class outcomes.

Agility is a critical business enabler that will help you build an organisation that can:

· evolve
· accelerate
· scale.

If you choose growth as your agility WHY, remember to give it a clear metric. If you don't there will be too many interpretations of what 'growth' means. Provide clarity with a meaningful measure.

Some other WHYs

Here are a few other WHYs for you to consider:

· **Customer-centricity:** Transform your organisation to put the customer at the centre.

- **Innovation:** Bring innovation to life in your organisation as your growth engine.
- **Waste reduction:** Reduce costs so you can scale effectively.
- **Culture change:** Turn a toxic culture into an enabling environment for all.
- **Speed:** Focus on getting into market fast to stay ahead of the competition.

CONNECTING AGILITY TO BUSINESS GROWTH

The critical relationship between business growth and agility

Innovation is critical to business growth and essential to stay competitive in an ever-changing and increasingly demanding world. Organisations need to dedicate a portion of their funding to innovation and ensure it does not compete based on the same guidelines as core business. The failure rate on an innovation pipeline should be a lot higher than your mature core business. You need to try things that are unproven, which can lead to volatile and unpredictable results. This is a positive, not a negative, and any innovation team who isn't failing is lying or isn't actually innovating. Key ingredients for business growth are value + innovation + speed + scale.

Innovation

The core of agile innovation is making small-value bets to prove something is a good idea before redirecting your company off other ideas (opportunity cost). Prove your idea first.

Innovation is littered with failure. In fact, organisations that excel in innovation frequently have a 90% failure rate on their innovation stream; for example, Amazon, Airbnb, booking.com. Companies not used to this need to adjust slowly.

Speed

If you have proven an idea works and will add value, you need to optimise how to deliver it. You need to make it as cheap as possible. So, baseline, track and optimise speed before scaling it. It is critical to do this on a small scale – if you don't you are introducing a resource-intensive innovation that will chew up profit, which defeats the purpose of the growth in the first place.

Scale

If you can't scale your innovation, you cannot make money and grow. Scaling is a critical stage in business growth and it is where the profit comes from.

HOW TO PUT THE WHY INTO YOUR AGILITY JOURNEY

You should have some ideas about what your WHY can be before you start your agility journey. Remember, always focus your people here. Do not let them get distracted by the HOW. You must:

- understand WHY you want to transform your organisation with agility
- rank and prioritise what problems you want to solve and how you will measure success
- start small and prove with evidence that you can make something add value in your organisation
- baseline, track and trend progress with metrics.

*

The next section of the book will lean into helping you understand the three organisational muscles for agility (refer to chapter 3) and which fitness workouts will help you build your muscles. Remember, it's important to use targeted tactics to get stronger and fitter.

CHAPTER 5

<u>HOW</u> – GETTING STARTED ON AGILITY

'THE BEST WAY TO PREDICT
THE FUTURE IS TO CREATE IT.'

PIONEERING COMPUTER
SCIENTIST ALAN KAY

TIME TO MAKE YOUR ORGANISATION AGILITY FIT

The first few chapters of this book explained why in a volatile, uncertain, complex and ambiguous world, businesses can no longer rely on traditional long-term strategic direction setting to succeed and grow. Today, organisations need to be able to quickly identify emerging changes in the marketplace and respond with speed to take advantage of potential opportunities or to counter rising threats. Digital technology has also changed the nature of work. It is transforming how and where work gets done and how many people are needed to do it.

The evidence is clear. Adaptive enterprises that have digital-led strategies and organisational agility have better chances of surviving and outperforming their competitors, and higher people retention. Forrester research shows that, on average, adaptive firms grow 3.2 times their industry average.[29] MIT research suggests that agile firms grow revenue 37% faster and generate 30% more profits than non-agile firms.[30]

If you want to succeed you need to sidestep the most common failures. If you need to remind yourself, go back and read the most common mistakes in chapter 1. Remember, agile is not a framework or a set of ceremonies or sprints or standups or sticky notes. Agile is simply a way of working to achieve your business goals quicker and cheaper.

How to make your organisation fit from an agility perspective:

1. Find your WHY.
2. Baseline your results with evidence and find areas that need improvement with the agility fitness test.
3. Create an agility fitness plan and custom design your agility journey:
   - uncover weak areas that need strengthening using feedback from the fitness assessment
   - use the three muscle groups: Outcomes, Behaviours, Mastery
   - pick and choose the workouts that align with areas that need strengthening
   - baseline, track and trend current your state and metrics
   - start your workout
   - re-baseline every six weeks.

This part of the book is all about HOW to successfully implement agility.

In chapter 3 you discovered there are three key organisational muscle groups to enterprise-wide agility:

· Outcomes – first, fast and frequent.
· Behaviours – behavioural change to build a high-growth and high-performance culture.
· Mastery – building a continuous self-learning organisation.

All three are critical to achieving agility success. Each group serves a different purpose and each has a set of discrete workouts to help build it and make it strong. 'Fit for purpose' is the key message, and every organisation is different, so which muscle groups you work on depends on your organisation, and you may need to try multiple workouts.

We'll now see how to use these muscle groups to successfully bring agility into your organisation. I provide an overview of each in this chapter, then we'll deep dive into all three in chapters 6, 7 and 8.

OUTCOMES (ORGANISATIONAL AGILITY MUSCLE GROUP #1)

Achieving business outcomes – first, fast and frequent

Customer value must be #1

Your organisation exists for a reason. It meets a need for customers and customers are happy to pay for it. This is not a static need; it is an ever-evolving need. However, as organisations get bigger and become organised into functional silos, customers and how you meet their needs and why they pay for it can become invisible to people; for example, a developer whose job is 'to build software', or a finance manager who 'just produces the monthly reports'. When this happens, it's easy for people to continue producing 'outputs' without any consideration of if they should, and does it add value and what would happen if they stopped doing so? In fact, organisations frequently at the top are focused on functional roles rather than being customer-centric.

Too many silos

So when your organisation gets larger and too functional and siloed and every team is meeting their own KPIs, the organisation easily gets fragmented. Every function and team pushes and moves in different directions; nothing happens quickly and everyone is too busy, and you can only seem to manage to get the organisation's priorities down to 30 to 50 things.

With all this organisational noise, it becomes impossible for people on the ground to 'know what good is'. Frequently the answer is 'everything', which invariably means people work on the wrong things.

The need to be adaptive

Organisations need to be adaptive because:

- customer needs change over time
- new competitors can potentially offer your services better and cheaper than you
- there is a need to increase revenue and profit by finding new customers.

Workouts to strengthen this muscle group

Organisations that have a strong Outcomes muscle group understand how they deliver value to their customers and why their customers choose them over a competitor. All functions and teams are pointing in the same direction and working on the agreed priorities of the customers while achieving ROI and exploring potential new customers and needs.

Organisations that have a weak or underdeveloped Outcomes muscle group need to utilise IMPACT – a set of workouts to strengthen the organisational Outcomes muscles. Each letter solves a different problem and gives a new skill.

Organisational muscle group	Workout series
Outcomes – first, fast and frequent	**I** – Inspire with a north star **M** – Measure what matters **P** – Prove don't assume **A** – Accelerate time to value **C** – Cadence, fast and frequent **T** – Transparency

Making your Outcomes muscles stronger and fitter is critical to organisational agility. The Outcomes muscle group is about pointing everyone in the same direction and reducing their baggage to allow them to move at pace. When everyone is facing the same direction, the next thing is to work out the Behaviours muscle group. This will help everyone work together successfully to build a high-performance team.

BEHAVIOURS (ORGANISATIONAL AGILITY MUSCLE GROUP #2)

Change behaviours to change cultures

People over processes and tools

It is impossible to transform an organisation if people do not change their behaviours. Most transformations focus on *processes* not *people*, because changing people is hard and confronting. However, people must change or you will fail. It would be like planting a new flower into unfertilised soil; it will certainly die and not grow.

Tip of the iceberg

The reason people don't change their behaviours is they simply don't know how. You need to show them, teach them, train them and role model good. Toxic cultures start at the top. Just own it. Leaders in organisations judge what they see, but people are always nice to leaders and you need to view what you are seeing as the tip of the iceberg. Obviously people are not showing you what's beneath the surface. Be conscious of this. You are definitely not getting the full picture and you are seeing what other people allow you to see.

High-performance teams

Organisations that have strong Behaviours muscles understand that success is utilising the brainpower of everyone in the organisation not just the select few at the top. This is true high performance. You need to utilise your most expensive asset to the max. This does not mean bleeding the team dry; it means energising them, allowing them to feel valued, giving them purpose and teaching them mastery.

The problems that this muscle group is solving are Patrick Lencioni's five dysfunctions of a team, shown below. A weak Behaviours muscle group organisation will be displaying these characteristics:

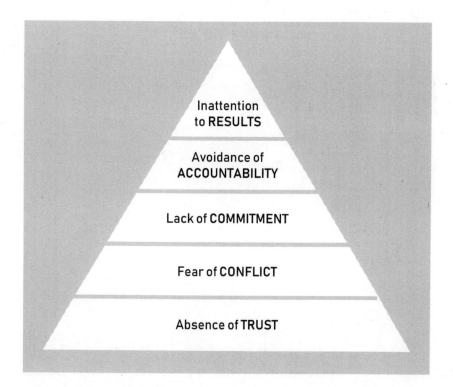

Workouts to strengthen this muscle group

If an organisation has a weak or underdeveloped Behaviours muscle group, it needs FACES workouts. Each letter solves a different problem and gives your people a new skill.

Organisational muscle group	Workout series
Behaviours – behavioural-led cultural change	**F** – Make FEEDBACK normal **A** – ACCOUNTABILITY with radical candour **C** – Healthy CONFLICT management **E** – ENERGY multipliers and drainers **S** – SELF-AWARENESS

The third organisational muscle group you need is Mastery. Exercising this muscle group will turn your organisation into a self-learning and growing organisation.

MASTERY (ORGANISATIONAL AGILITY MUSCLE GROUP #3)

Scale by becoming a continuously evolving organisation

Don't underestimate the learning curve

Organisations and people frequently:

- underestimate the path to mastery
- overestimate their own capability
- don't understand how people retain, retrieve and apply information
- underestimate the power of learning together rather than as individuals.

If you can't solve these problems, your organisation will not be equipped to transform into fast and adaptive. When this happens, organisations tend to implement new change and skills badly. Frequently they have never seen what 'good looks like' and they learn bad habits from others upfront. People need to know what good looks like and how to know when they have achieved it.

Become a continuous self-learning organisation

Organisations that have strong Mastery muscles understand the path to mastery is multi-tiered, and how you learn a skill at the start of this mastery journey and how you improve that skill at a later part of that journey is different. Mastery is a team not an individual activity. Also, organisations must embed self-learning and growing. The organisation must grow like a living organism, which means constant and structured learning. It must occur effortlessly and naturally, with a focus on helping other teams succeed so that everyone can have success.

Mastery muscles

If organisations have a weak or underdeveloped Mastery muscle group, they must understand Broadwell's four stages of learning as a structured path to mastery. In 1969, Matthew Broadwell designed the four stages of learning that everyone must go through to get to mastery. A structured approach to mastery is key. It takes time to achieve mastery and to guide people through each of the levels.

Workouts to strengthen this muscle group

There are four levels to mastery. You can't skip them. You need to transition through them all.

Organisational muscle group	Workout series
Mastery – building a continuous learning organisation	L1 – Role model – observation L2 – Learn by doing – assisted L3 – Learn by doing – unassisted L4 – Role model for others

TIME TO WORK OUT!

Organisational agility is achieved by working on these three muscle groups together for success. As with all fitness training, you should baseline your muscle strength. You also will need to get targeted. Choose the right workouts to build the muscles groups effectively to solve your specific organisational weaknesses.

To use the rest of the book successfully, first take the agility fitness test if you haven't done so already (refer to chapter 3). This will help you decide what areas need the most improvement and where to start. With your agility fitness test results, you can cherrypick which workouts you should try and what parts of the organisational muscle they are improving. This is a very targeted approach that will deliver quick wins for you and your teams.

Let's get started!

CHAPTER 6
<u>HOW</u> – OUTCOMES FIRST, FAST AND FREQUENT

'THE ONLY PLACE WHERE SUCCESS COMES BEFORE WORK IS THE DICTIONARY.'

VINCE LOMBARDI

WORKOUTS TO BUILD YOUR OUTCOMES AGILITY MUSCLE GROUP

Let's get started

This chapter contains a set of workouts designed to strengthen and build your Outcomes muscles. Ideally, you will have completed the agility fitness test so that you know which workouts to prioritise. There are six workouts in total, as shown in the following table. Each letter solves a different problem and gives you a new skill.

Problem you need to solve		How to solve it – workouts
Lacking clarity, too many organisational priorities	I	Inspire with a north star
Organisational goals are not measurable	M	Measure what matters
Projects not delivering benefits	P	Prove don't assume
Taking too long to get an idea into market	A	Accelerate time to market
Your organisation is lacking an operational rhythm	C	Cadence, fast and frequent
Paper status reporting, frequently inaccurate	T	Transparency

Going for gold

- Custom-design your agility journey by picking which workouts will deliver quick wins.
- Baseline your starting position with evidence and metrics.
- Reflect every six weeks; what has made a difference?
- Adapt, rerun and embed what's working well.

IMPACT – INSPIRE WITH A NORTH STAR

Direction is much more important than speed – some are going nowhere fast

Who

This workout is for you if the following are familiar to you:

- Volume – too many objectives/priorities.
- Complexity – objectives and priorities are set at every level of the organisation.
- Priority setting – priorities are conflicting and/or everything is a high priority.
- Alignment – objectives and priorities do not link to the work.
- New way of working – OKRs (objectives and key results) implemented but everyone still is confused.
- Under-communicating and/or passive (one way) communications with your people.
- Unbalanced portfolio with no focus on growth or innovation.

One of the biggest problems organisations (and their employees) face is a lack of clarity:

- **What** are we aiming for?
- **How** will we know when we achieve it?
- **Where** do I fit in helping the organisation achieve it?

Why

Focus

Most agile journeys fail before they are completed. The journey is normally initiated because the organisation wishes to transform into something different, yet there is a lack of clarity or purpose on what that is and why it is needed. The focus is generally on sprints, standups and ceremonies. Frequently teams deliver new features and functionality to customers, but are they adding value? How do you know? How do you measure? Rolling out an agile framework without a business goal in mind will mean your rollout will lack purpose and direction. It is much better to decide on what your organisational goal is and to then think about HOW.

You need to always have a north star and take a long view of the future. Creating clarity on the north star allows you to make smarter and more responsible decisions.

An agility transformation must be tied to clear and measurable organisational outcomes. Tactics not anchored to an outcome are destined to fail. So if your organisation lacks focus and clarity, spend time figuring out your north star and using a north star metric.

Why do organisations have too many priorities?

I love this question, because frequently it is a sign that the executive team are not working as a team but as individuals. Everyone has their pet project and, instead of challenging them or creating alignment, the simplest solution is to agree to prioritise them all. If an executive team is not working as one team, they do not prioritise. What they seem to miss is the consequence of this – it means the organisation is going nowhere fast and people end up working on the wrong things. Executives must take accountability when this happens.

What is a north star?

Clarity and purpose are critical for success and this means understanding your organisation's north star. A north star, just like Polaris, is the brightest star in the sky. It is a well-defined marker to help you navigate through darkness and uncertainty. A north star is your organisation's orienting point – your fixed point in a constantly changing marketplace – that helps you stay on track as an organisation. It is the internal compass, unique to your organisation, that represents why your organisation exists and what value you will deliver to your customers.

North star versus objectives or OKRs

It is not one or the other. In my experience, a north star is simply your top OKR. I choose the language of north star because organisations frequently get distracted and put in too many objectives or OKRs. Bringing the focus back to a north star will give you fewer OKRs and more focus.

Communication

Executive teams frequently underestimate how much communication is required to achieve clarity. Annual and quarterly town halls simply do not cut it. It is only when people on the ground understand how their role is applicable to the north star and how the organisation is tracking against it that you can say with comfort that everyone understands what the organisation is trying to achieve.

Where things go wrong in the creation of a north star

Pitfalls to watch for:

- meaningless platitudes, such as 'sell more units', 'more revenue', 'add value'
- the north star is not anchored in customer value or needs
- the north star is not grounded in reality or is not achievable
- the north star is directionless – it does not help with decisions and prioritising
- you have a great north star, but people don't know it or understand it.

The starting position for all organisations on their agile journey should be a north star and a direction. But it's not enough to have a north star – you need to have a good one.

This will not be the only metric that matters, but it is your guide.

What

A north star metric

If you have too many priorities, it is time to lean into fixing this. The best way I have seen this work is encouraging the executive team to pick one north star metric they all commit to as the top priority. *Hacking Growth* by Sean Ellis includes an approach that I find works quite well. He came up with the concept of a north star metric: the one metric to help provide direction to the people in your company and that all functions get behind.

A north star metric is the value your customer gets in return for the price they pay you – for example:

Company/product	North star metric
Uber	Rides per week
Spotify	Time spent listening
Airbnb	Booked nights
LinkedIn	Monthly active users
MS Teams	Daily active users
Netflix	Monthly viewing hours
Miro	Number of collaboration boards per business
YouTube	Minutes watched
Salesforce	Average records created per account

How to use this for success

Each initiative or strategy you run must be assessed to see how it will contribute to the north star metric. The intent of the metric is to help you prioritise and create focus. It isn't a north star metric if only 20% of your capacity is aligned to achieving it.

Communicating your north star metric

If you have solved the problem of priority and have a clear north star, the next issue is communicating it in your organisation so that everyone understands it. The north star must be communicated in multiple ways and many times before the people in your organisation will actually start to understand what it is. Communicating the north star is a two-way communication. The CEO and the executive team must start the direction with a north star and then they must listen to their people to see if the message has been understood.

Tactics

There are four different tactics to creating focus and clarity in your organisation:

Focus	Define your north star to guide everyone *before* setting objectives.
Direction	Use obeya as your GPS to your north star.
Engagement	Bring your vision to life for your people with experientials.
Gemba walks	Spend time with people as they work – observe, learn, and get feedback.

Let's look at each of these.

FOCUS – Define your north star to guide everyone *before* setting objectives

Create clarity in your organisation by defining a north star metric. Make it visible, embed it in all communications, and track progress against it. Get everyone in the organisation to understand it.

Who are you targeting, and what problem are you solving? How can you do it uniquely?

- Customer – define your customer success moment.
- Measurement – can you measure it?
- Time – define a time range with enough frequency.
- Control – is the metric within your control?
- Growth – if this metric grows will your business grow?

Then baseline, track, trend, validate and create a feedback loop.

What is *not* a north star metric:

- revenue
- profit
- internal processes.

These are secondary measures.

Your north star must represent WHY your customers buy from you.[*]

---

[*] Recommended resource: Amplitude, www.miro.com/app/board/uXjVPf0HwEA=.

How will you know when you have achieved it?

- The organisation must have a clear north star that is measurable and tracked.
- The north star must be used to prioritise work to be done.

DIRECTION – Use obeya as your GPS to your north star

If you have a north star and have managed to reduce your priorities, it is time to create a map based on the north star. What strategies will you prioritise, what people and funding will be assigned to them, and are they tracking and trending in the right direction or do you need to stop and try something else?

When teams scale to over 250 people, staying on top of everything becomes complex:

- What is everyone working on?
- Is the work to be done aligned to corporate vision and strategy?
- Does everyone understand how they 'fit' from a value perspective and their role?
- Is everyone working on things of the highest value?
- Are people delivering value or outputs?

In my experience, obeya is the best way to understand the answers to these questions.

At its core, 'obeya' (Japanese for 'big room') is a lean manufacturing tool in which a dedicated room is set aside for people to meet and make decisions about a specific topic or problem. It sounds simple, but a dedicated obeya can have far-reaching impacts in the workplace that enhance productivity, save money, increase efficiency and improve communication. The idea behind an obeya is to break down the barriers that prevent employees from collaborating and sharing information to make efficient decisions.

Obeya provides:

- transparency and insight into the health of the organisation
- the ability to accelerate decision-making
- the ability to see, learn and act together
- the ability to build high-performance teams
- alignment for leaders and teams.

A physical room obeya is powerful. It provides an anchor to the team – I usually have all my team and customer meetings in such a room. People *love* to browse the wall and ask questions. Encourage it.

ENGAGEMENT – Bring your vision to life for your people with experientials

The biggest challenge I frequently see in organisations is that they have a purpose, mission, objectives, metrics ... *yet* ... the people on the ground simply do not understand any of it. It's not real to them at all. So they cannot relate and, therefore, it is not important nor does it guide their work.

So how can you solve this problem and bring your north star to life? The best way to share with your team is to create an experiential activation of the future.

There are two types of experientials:

- **Physical activation experientials:** Create a real-life physical space that shows the north star from a customer perspective in the future.
- **Digital prototype experientials:** Showcase what the experience will be for customers in the future.

Characteristics of an experiential activation include:

- it is tactile – a hands-on or interactive experience
- it has active engagement not passive engagement (watching a video, reading a memo)
- it is customer-centric – the customer is at the centre of the activation
- it has time horizons – there must be a connection with the future and a relevant timeline. Having people work on something in the next 18 months but showing them something from 10 years in the future is not helpful. It won't create the clarity required.

An experiential is the way to go to create excitement and to bring life to your north star!

GEMBA WALKS – Spend time with people as they work – observe, learn and get feedback

Gemba is Japanese for 'site' or 'scene'. A gemba walk is a great way for leaders of an organisation to connect with people doing their work.

The best way for this to happen is for leaders to go to the people and the work. A leader being visible is critical to organisational success and will help people in the organisations see that you are invested in making them a success and care enough to see what challenges they face when they perform their role.

Typically the CEO will walk through the value-creating process in their organisation so that they can see and experience firsthand what happens, rather than taking their information from a sanitised PowerPoint pack. The CEO walks through the process to understand how the business is actually working. It is about getting out of the office and into the process with the organisation's people to help them discuss issues and fix them.

The gemba walk helps senior leaders build relationships with the rest of the organisation and is a fundamental tactic to improving teamwork and the effectiveness of teams.

The key elements of a gemba walk are:

- Observe only – don't correct or modify activities during the walk.
- Seek to understand – why do people perform the task this way?
- Investigate value adds – find the value-add activities.
- Find value deficits – where are you losing value in the existing process? Why?
- Encourage innovation – improve conditions, tools and procedures and remove items that are detrimental.

A gemba walk is usually the quickest way for a senior leader to fully grasp the pain points of an organisation because you get to experience them firsthand. A PowerPoint pack cannot deliver the same impact.

Wins

- **Focus:** Your entire company, regardless of function or role, has the same metric. Wow!
- **Customer:** The customer is at the centre of everything you do.
- **Purpose:** The whole organisation has a strong sense of purpose, which fuels motivation.
- **Engagement:** Your team is engaged and excited.

Real-life case study – when doing less is the win

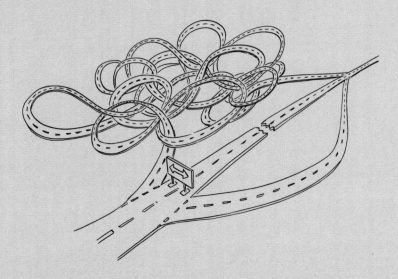

Organisations moving to agile seem to love OKRs (objectives and key results) – they deep dive into them straightaway. The most common problem is too many OKRs – hence the need for a north star metric.

Problem

An Australian insurance company reached out to me. They had a $200M project and it was 16 weeks before go live. The CEO had committed to media and a launch date. However, they were code red. This was an agile environment, but with a very immature understanding of agile: 'we can change requirements any time we want and still have it completed in time'. I was asked to enable the new product to launch on the agreed date – and to ensure the product was awesome.

Approach

My first step was to make work and flow of work visible. They had seven different product teams flowing work into one technology build team. My assessment was 20% of the features were DONE, 20% were in QA and 60% were still in ideation stage. They were indeed a code red! Drastic change was required to bring this in on time. The political landscape was tense with people looking to lay blame.

Observation

The build team were overwhelmed and were trying to please everyone. As a consequence, they had set up no boundaries for success and defining what good was. Most of them were contractors and they were about to walk.

Solution

I needed to slow the flow of work down. Each day, I started making visible the number of features waiting on business approval, signing and testing. I introduced trends for these stats to show that they were increasing, not decreasing. We introduced silly celebrations and rewards for business teams that had trends that were decreasing. This put a focus on finishing as opposed to starting. We changed the dynamic of power to encourage product teams to spend their time completing features rather than putting in new features. I called this changing the conversation by stealth. This approach enabled us to go live on the agreed date, on budget, but with only 50% of the feature set. Yet, the product won an industry award and on go live no one noticed the missing features.

Reflection

Organisations frequently want teams to do more, pushing people to burn out and creating toxic cultures without really leaning into what adds the most value.

Way forward

I recommend organisations reorient their three- to five-year north star every quarter. Things change. That's okay. Get into a repeatable process where everyone knows the first week of the quarter the north star orientation. It is also important to assess – are we still on track? Or did we get lost? Again, both answers are fine once you reorient yourself back on track. Remember, all journeys have changes due to unforeseen traffic and roadworks. Just acknowledge them and move forward.

If you now have a north star, you have completed your first workout to making your Outcomes muscles fitter and stronger. This is a good fitness foundation. This workout is all about reducing confusion in organisations by putting metrics and evidence down to represent progress and success rather than relying on opinions. You're getting ready to be evidence-based!

IMPACT – MEASURE WHAT MATTERS

Move away from opinions to evidence and fact-based decisions

Who

We started with workout **I – Inspire with your north star**, which will define success and provide direction and help guide your teams on what customers need and want. Next is **M – Measure what matters**. This workout is all about using evidence and metrics to ensure you stay on track. You need to baseline where you are with evidence, and orient yourself with evidence along the way.

This workout is for you if the following is familiar to you:

- Evidence – opinions and emotions are how decisions get made.
- Alignment – there is a lack of clarity as to what work links to what metric.
- Capacity – there is a lack of understanding on capacity assigned to what metric.
- Complexity – too many metrics, too much confusion.
- Improvement – you don't know if your organisation is getting better or worse quarter on quarter.

What you will learn in this workout:

- Customer value – tracking value to your north star metric is #1.
- Customer behaviour metrics – tracking customer feature usage and frequency for ROI comes next.
- Learning metrics – knowing what to track outside of value.
- Visualisation and trends – essential for engagement and understanding.

- Data and centralised dashboards – critical instead of paper-based opinions.
- Actionable insights – metrics are only useful when you review together as a team with action.

Why

How would you train for a marathon or to lose weight?

To improve in any arena, you need to track data and decide on metrics. A simple analogy would be deciding you wanted to lose 10kg and get fit. A strategy to achieve your outcome is to eat healthily and train for a half marathon with a finish time of 1 hour 45 minutes; however, today you are overweight and have never run more than one kilometre. So how do you get started? It will make sense to invest in a smartwatch such as a Fitbit or a Garmin to help you assess your journey and to help you understand how achievable your goal is. Then, like most things, you just need to start small, by running smaller distances and reducing your food intake.

Tracking your performance is a journey. What you track depends on what stage you are currently in. For example, when you get started, performance tracking upfront is very crude. You might start tracking how many days you run and how long each run is. As you get fitter, you will want to move to more sophisticated tracking, such as heart rate threshold, pace and split times.

Data and evidence is the start of the conversation not the outcome

Organisations are no different. How do you decide what you should track? To get started, you need to think about what you wish to achieve and what the current stage of your journey is. It can seem overwhelming to decide upfront. The first step is transparency; make your work visible and 'listen' to the data by tracking trends daily or weekly. The intent is to use the data to drive conversations and debate. The data is the start of the conversation, not the outcome. You need the data because 'act, measure, adapt' is so important for performance, and without the data you cannot assess where to focus your energy and why.

Encourage open conversation on why the trends are moving the way they are and if you should change your behaviour or actions.

High-performance teams

High-performance teams do things differently to give themselves an edge over their competitors. This applies equally to enterprise transformations as it does to ironman competitors. A person training for an ironman who wishes to have the edge will measure their performance and calibrate their program to optimise their outcome. If you want to stand out from your competitors, you need to get used to measuring how you are doing. This is not to say metrics are the be-all and end-all of everything, but you will get useful data that may cause you to tweak your approach or path to success.

Opinion is still the 'norm'

I am a big fan of being data and evidence driven. I am quite shocked how many organisations still utilise unvalidated opinion over data to make decisions and to decide what to prioritise. Also due to hierarchies and the size of organisations, this opinion becomes an organisational whisper up the company levels, and at each stage it is misinterpreted and changed to please a stakeholder or receiver of the information. So much so that when it reaches the top it no longer resembles the original message!

Cultural change

The biggest surprise with becoming data and evidence driven is that it is mostly a cultural change. Most teams fear measurement and data because they worry it will be used against them. So don't be surprised if the resistance level is high on implementing a data-driven and evidence-based approach. The best way to embed the culture is to reward visibility, and tracking and trending over improvements. Rewarding the right behaviours is essential to embed any change and take on people's concerns. If they track and trend and become data driven, don't use the data against them. If you want 10x growth, data driven is the only way to go, so give people safety to understand the power of tracking data and metrics.

A data-driven culture means instilling trust and commitment among all the members of an organisation to collaborate fluidly together on shared metrics by enabling access to data at their fingertips.

Organisations today

Most organisations have performance cycles and objectives for their teams in place so they feel that they don't have any work to do here. However, in my experience the measurement process implemented is poorly executed or understood. The most consistent phrase I hear at the moment is, 'We have OKRs so we are doing great' … but that sentence does not actually mean anything or say anything.

OKRs v north star v measures that matter

Let's dig deep on language. In my experience, OKRs is the performance system most in use today and when used well, it rocks! So I am a supporter.

Measure What Matters by John Doerr is a great book. This book introduced the concept of OKRs – objectives and key results:

- **Objectives** are meant to be long lived and align more with **I – Inspire with a north star**.
- **Key Results** are shorter term (often quarterly) and align more with **M – Measure what matters**.

I split the O and KR because frequently people don't understand that the O and the KR are different.

Google is the biggest supporter of this system. When understood and used properly, OKRs are a valuable tool for insight; however, frequently that is not the case. I recommend sticking with 'north star' and 'measure what matters' to guide you on HOW to set your OKRs successfully.

When it goes wrong

OKRs are a big buzzword in organisations today. Everyone wants to know what your OKR is, and the assumption is if I call something an OKR then I must be succeeding at work.

But most of the time, I have seen OKRs not work. At all. This is about OKR implementation and knowledge not OKRs themselves.

So, do not assume OKRs are a silver bullet. They are not. Most of the time they are implemented badly and add little value and, in fact, end up confusing teams. Challenges I frequently see with OKR setting include:

- Too many OKRs – an avalanche of OKRs (in the hundreds) and set at every level.
- Lack of clarity – conflicting OKRs and everyone is thinking their OKR is most important.
- Badly written objectives – vague objectives that have been written *after* the HOW.
- Key results that don't help – key results that don't measure anything useful and are not time specific.
- Lack of relevance – most of the time, the people doing the work don't even pay attention to their OKRs.
- Lack of understanding or training on OKRs and what a good one is.
- Lack of alignment to capacity and how people spend their time.

OKRs that change quarterly and don't track progress against objectives are not helpful, and nor do they provide insight.[*]

What

So what does 'measure what matters' mean to me? The following are the key areas that organisations care about today and I recommend you measure:

- **Customer and business value:**
  - Are we meeting customers' needs? North star + CSAT (customer satisfaction) + fast feedback loops.
  - Profit & Loss, ROI. What does it cost to meet customers' needs?
- **Predictability:** What did we say, and what did we do? This assists forecasting and likely ending position.
- **Productivity:** Are we reducing time and cost to market?
- **Agility:** How frequently are we putting change in customer hands (deployment frequency)?

---

[*] For more on this, go to www.hbs.edu/ris/Publication%20Files/09-083.pdf.

- **Stability and quality:** Are products free of defects and issues?
- **Happiness:** Are our people happy or are they at risk of burnout?
- **Growth:** Is the organisation growing and learning? Or stagnating?

Four things to watch for when deciding to measure something:

1. Focus	Do your OKRs help your team understand what is and – more importantly – what isn't important?
2. Align	OKRs must have a direct relationship to work being done. There must be 100% alignment. Frequently organisations only use OKRs for change initiatives and not all work. People should *only* be working on things that map to an OKR.
3. Track	Data and not opinions. You must be able to assess progress. You should frequently assess the need for things to be validated or improved. I frequently see objectives drafted once and not improved. Everyone knows they don't make sense but decide to ignore them rather than make them better.
4. Stretch	North star provides direction and must be inspirational.

To have real IMPACT you need to learn to make tough choices, and to keep your team on track you need to track their progress and measure what matters.

Objectives are WHAT will be achieved. They should be concrete and action oriented.

Key Results benchmark and monitor HOW you and your team gets to the objective. They are specific and time-bound and realistic and achievable. Frequently they are quarterly time limited.

They should be used with 100% transparency and a data-driven approach.

Tactics

M – Measure what matters has four important components:

1. Data – the evidence of what you are tracking, not opinions.
2. Visualisation – how you communicate the evidence and trend it so people can get insights.
3. Discussion – insights are not straightforward, so discussing them is critical.
4. Actionable insight – having insights without action is a waste of time, so track an action plan.

Data

You need to consider:

- **Value:**
  - North star metric.
  - CSAT:
    - ~ Companies frequently measure CSAT; however, you *must* create a relationship between the customer journey, CSAT and changes made recently.
    - ~ Fast feedback loops – so many organisations talk about fast feedback loops, but are all talk and no action. It simply means the ability to track the performance and usage of a feature or change in the market. This is super powerful for prioritising the *right* things to work on.
  - You must create a relationship between work done and feedback from the market.

- **Predictability:** Teams hate this one, but it is sobering and essential – this is all about accountability and learning.

  It is amazing how many organisations today have OKRs but don't track success against them! I utilise this simple measure quarterly: what did you say you would do, and what did you do?

  Another term is 'planned to done'.

It is not designed to be a stick; it is designed to be a learning measure. When teams start measuring for the first time, it is not unusual for success to be less than 50%. This simply means that they were too ambitious or had too many things to do.

Predictability is a useful measure for future forecasting. I have seen teams use it to narrow scope if they predict a launch date too far out.

- **Productivity:** Reducing time or cost to market. Most organisations today *do not* track how long it takes or costs to get something to market! I think it is because they are afraid to. I deep dive on this in **A – Accelerate time to value**.

  The best measures are lead and cycle times. I recommend baselining, finding your biggest bottlenecks and removing them, and tracking the impact.

- **Stability and quality:** Reducing cost and speed to market should not be at the expense of stability and quality and compliance. When delivering change to customers, it is important to ensure quality of service is not impacted. Escaped defect rate – number of defects post deployment – is the most common measure.

- **Happiness:** This is all about your people, and as a consequence is your most important measure. Are your people happy? Do they have too much work to do?

  I like simple measures for this – for example, rate 1–5 happiness, five things to improve, five things to not change. Are we getting better and taking action from feedback?

- **Growth:** Is the organisation growing and learning?

  Business growth should use the north star metrics. Is your organisation learning (I deep dive into this more later). There are four stages of learning with the intent that best-in-class teams role model for others.

  I love this system and I have used it successfully, and it is also easy to track teams going through different stages of the learning journey and then the number of teams role modelling for others.

Visualisation

To understand the data, visualisation is critical. It makes data easier for the human brain to understand and pull insights from. The main goal of data visualisation is to make it easier to identify patterns, trends and outliers. Data visualisation will assist with speed of decision-making because it will be easier to spot trends, negative or positive, which will enable you to act on them more quickly.

Today tools such as PowerBI and Thoughtspot make visualisation quick and cheap. You no longer need specialised skills to bring the data to life. The goal is to keep it simple; the data stays in the source system and you aggregate it centrally using one of these tools.

Discussion + data quality = actionable insight

Data without discussion is pointless. The reason you are tracking the data is to learn and assess what it's telling you so you can action it. The purpose of data and discussions is to help you decide what to do next. Encourage debate and discussion. Data has many lenses and interpretations, and the goal is to have actionable insights that you track and validate. Discussions should be weekly, and should be included into any continuous improvement sessions so the improvements can be validated.

One thing to note: when you start discussing the data, you will lean into accuracy and quality of the data – you must see this as a journey because it takes time to get high-quality data. Spot any accuracy issues and take action to improve the data input. You will need to have spot checks for quality.

Integrate metrics and work to be done

Tracking metrics and evidence and trends must be connected to work to be done. The work to be done should be moving the dial on the metrics or it is the wrong work. Don't make the mistake of separating metrics, evidence, work to be done and capacity. This is the 'system of work' – it is interconnected. Do not track in silos; track in small integrated packages.

Wins

- **CSAT uplift:** Taking feedback from the market and using it to deliver what customers want.
- **Productivity uplift:** By removing guessing and assumptions, you will improve the right things.
- **Focus:** Ensure people can relate what they are working on to a measure.
- **Engagement:** Everyone can see how what they are doing has a direct impact on bottom line.
- **Progress:** Are you heading in the right direction? If not, you need to course correct.

Real-life case study – the power of making work visible

Problem

I was brought in by the CIO of a Top 4 bank. He was frustrated because his team of 600 people had made minimal progress on their top 22 'change' initiatives over the past 12 months. I was told the bottleneck was their agile experience. They had moved to new way ways of working 18 months ago and everything was stuck. I was asked to uplift their agile delivery skillset.

Approach

So, I got started by engaging with the 40 squads. I spent time understanding what each squad did and we started to map their flow of work and all the work currently in progress. We did this virtually using Confluence and Jira. I needed to introduce a common language across the squads so that we could see the system of work and spot patterns.

Observations

When we did this, it was apparent that the problem was not that the teams needed help going faster; the issue was that they had too much work on their plates. The predictability rating for the quarter was 20%! Why? 80% of their work queue was run/operational work or regulatory and only 20% capacity was the top 22 change initiatives. So there was a lack of alignment between what the CIO wanted and the work they were doing. This was a problem at the CIO end; you cannot ignore 80% of people's work queues. Also, each squad had their own PO (product owner) and each of the 40 squads created their own work queues and priorities, leading to gridlock.

Solution

We solved the problem by capping capacity and reducing priorities. We capped run/regulatory work from 80% of the pipeline to 50% of the pipeline and we uplifted the change initiative pipeline from 20% to 50%. I also worked with the CIO to reduce the top 22 priorities to a top three priorities. Within six months the top three priorities were 100% complete and the squads could move to the next set of priorities.

Reflection

Making work and flow visible highlighted the real bottlenecks. I could have easily not validated the remit and just dived straight into solution mode. If I had taken that approach, I would not have solved the problem. I frequently find the original remit and the root cause are different, so I always validate. It is a superpower. The power of making everything visible is that we found the real problem, and then we could fix it.

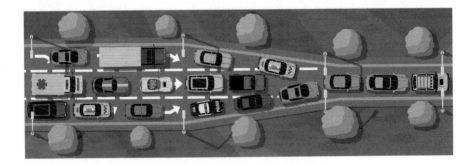

Way forward

Don't get too hung up on getting the metrics right upfront. Start quickly, use evidence, make it visible. You will mature your understanding over time on what is a good metric and what isn't. The most important thing is to build the habit of evidence over opinions and get people to focus on achieving a metric rather than getting lost in the work that is never-ending.

*

So we are two workouts in and your Outcomes muscles are getting stronger. You have a north star that is pointing everyone in the same direction. This workout was all about evidence and metrics rather than opinions. This will help your organisation assess progress on the journey to the north star.

The next workout for the Outcomes muscle group is **P – Prove don't assume**. This is all about transforming the work you do and how you do it. The work you do and where your team spends their time is expensive. It is important you do not waste such a valuable resource. So this workout is all about constantly validating that what you are doing will deliver the results and outcomes you need. You do this with small bets and experimentation.

IMPACT – PROVE DON'T ASSUME

Never assume anything

Who

Organisations are often run on executives' opinions, which are frequently unvalidated but assumed to be accurate. Unless you have validated and proved with evidence that your opinion will work in this instance, it is just an assumption. Moving from opinions to evidence is the fastest path to reducing costs and increasing focus. Frequently executives give teams too much work because they have not validated their opinions.

This workout is for you if the following is familiar to you:

- ROI – you are delivering lots of features, but customers or revenue is flatlining.
- Burnout – your team are unhappy and burnt out and you are frustrated with them.

- Budget – your teams keep asking for more budget but you are uncertain.
- Hamster wheel – the team is on a continual hamster wheel and getting nowhere fast.
- Paper business cases are your method of funding release.
- You never say no or stop work.
- You are asking teams to commit to work early when the least is known.

What you will learn in this workout:

- Small bets before large spend – learn how experimentation leads to wise spending.
- Experimentation – understand what it is and how to implement simply.
- Prioritisation – learn how to utilise experiments to prioritise based on value.
- Value – understand that if a customer is not using a feature, value is non-existent.
- Prove don't assume – use empiricism, experimentation and evidence.

Why

A few years ago I was brought in to lead a large $200 million program. The premise was to offer the current customer base a new loyalty program and marketplace, and we could then cross-sell another product to 25% of our existing base and double our revenue. For two years everyone was pumped, and of course what happened? The concept tanked within 12 months of launch, and two years later was discretely pushed to the side and never mentioned in the organisation again.

Another organisation I worked at paid exorbitant prices to a design consultancy to validate their own confirmation bias that if they made their product 'prettier' they could move it from a free service to a premium subscription service. They performed all sorts of focus groups but the questions and the frame of them were narrow and misleading, with only one outcome: great idea, please continue. They were wrong also.

I could go on and on. Ego is the biggest enemy here. Too many senior executives are willing to bet the farm on an idea that they really like without validating if their customers feel the same way.

So why do companies prefer to assume their idea is the next big thing when the odds are stacked against them? Or why would they prefer to pay a big consultancy millions to agree with their own confirmation bias rather than implement a test-and-learn approach?

In a *HBR* article 'Why Businesses Don't Experiment', author Dan Ariely stated that there are two main reasons for this:

- Experiments require short-term losses for long-term gains. Companies (and people) are notoriously bad at making those trade-offs.
- There is a false sense of security provided by 'experts'. When we pay consultants, we get an answer from them and not a list of experiments to conduct. We tend to value answers over questions because answers allow us to take action, while questions mean we need to keep thinking. Never mind that asking good questions and gathering evidence usually guides us to better answers.

So, you need to ask yourself, if the average lifespan of organisations is getting shorter and shorter and the pressure to adapt is ever stronger in today's market, why are you not experimenting more to ensure your company is not stagnating and not betting on the wrong horse? It is time to move away from ego and opinion and move to data and experimentation.

What

The best way to prioritise and reduce risk is with experimentation. Teams should be given 'seed funding' upfront to test, mature and prove their concepts. This approach of making small bets before making a big bet is the most likely way to succeed and get a good business outcome.

Everything you write should be treated as an unvalidated assumption until proven otherwise. This can transform your organisation and save your scarce budgets to spend on the right things.

Becoming data driven

Like everything, becoming data driven and utilising experimentation is a journey. I recommend starting with tracking user behaviour – don't just ask their opinion, track their behaviour. What features do they use? What is the frequency of the usage? What percentage of features get used? What doesn't get used? Start joining the dots on the cost for each feature and the value it delivers when measured by user behaviour and frequency of usage, to assess the ROI of each feature. You will gain some interesting insights. It is not uncommon for only 20% of the features you push to market to add any real value to customers.

Using fast feedback loops to prioritise your work queues

Take this data and look at the ideas you have in the pipeline. From what you have learnt from the data, which of your current ideas are most likely to succeed? Prioritise those.

Building hypotheses and experimenting

So how can you validate these prioritised ideas quickly and cheaply? Brainstorm.

Tactics

The model that I teach my teams to experiment and to move away from assumptions to evidences is the DIBB model – it is very simple.

Data, Insights, Beliefs, Bets (DIBB)

DIBB is an argument framework.

Data	Qualitative or quantitative information that informs a perspective. This should not be an interpretation.
Insights	What is your interpretation of the data? What have you learned?
Beliefs	Based on your interpretation, what beliefs have you formed about the problem space you are working in?
Bets	Based on your beliefs, what are the bets you should make?
Metric	What does success look like?

Example: Spotify

Data	How people were listening to music was changing. Desktop users were declining and mobile users were increasing. However, internally our teams were more focused on desktop rather than mobile users.
Insight	Mobile is overtaking desktop as the primary music gadget. We don't have enough mobile developers compared to desktop developers.
Belief	We have been optimising for the wrong thing. For long-term survival, we need to become mobile first.
Bet	Hire a bunch of mobile devs. Train the desktop devs to become mobile devs. Build infrastructure for iterating fast on mobile. Introduce feedback loop to validate data/continue DIBBs iteratively.

Companies using experimentation to enable their growth strategy include Airbnb, Amazon, Booking.com, Facebook, LinkedIn, Netflix, Spotify and Uber. Look into how innovation and decision-making works in each one of these companies and in other key players today.

Let's go over some of the reasons these companies take experimentation so seriously (and why you should, too):

· Experiments save you from potentially expensive mistakes.

· Experiments accelerate innovation.

· Experimentation accelerates decision-making. The certainty that an initiative will go through reliable validation reduces the discussions and bureaucracy keeping it from coming alive.

· Measuring the results of an effort is much easier. When there is no experimentation, it is common to see companies interrupting the work of senior professionals and even entire teams to try to understand the real impact that resulted from a change that was made recently. With A/B Testing, accurate results are accessible to everyone.

- Lastly, one of my favourites: with experimentation, you don't have to implement every new thing you do with the highest quality code, translated into every language, perfectly responsive in all devices, with complete documentation, and so on. While testing, you are concerned with implementing the minimum necessary to *validate your hypothesis*. You will only invest in everything you need for a final delivery if the experiments show that your hypothesis truly works. This can drastically increase a company's efficiency and productivity.

Real-life examples

My working life is littered with examples of companies not validating scope or approach. Examples of misguided beliefs that should have been tested and measured are:

- building a new deposit account for retail customers will attract new customers
- building a new deposit account before a 10-minute mortgage product is a cheap and good idea
- building a new bank on the side – adding more work – is better than stopping work
- giving our customers a loyalty program will make them more likely to stay
- building a marketplace will double our customer numbers.

Experimentation is hard. However, it is much easier than spending years and hundreds of millions of dollars and then realising two years after launch that something was a bad idea. It just requires people to state, 'My idea is an assumption. I really believe it will work, but I am humble enough to say I don't *know*. Why don't we check my assumptions are correct and spend 10% of the money validating before spending all of our cash on an idea that could be put on the scrap heap in two years?'

Way forward

We have completed three of the six workouts designed to make your organisational Outcomes muscle group stronger – well done! We have everyone using the north star to point in the right direction. We are using metrics to prove we are on the right path. We have started validating our assumptions on what direction we should take. What a strong start!

The next workout is about increasing the pace of the organisation. We need to move at speed. We need to identify what blockers are slowing us down and remove them. I want you to use evidence to show your speed is accelerating.

Let me show you how.

IMPACT – ACCELERATE TIME TO VALUE

Speed is the ultimate weapon in business. All else being equal, the fastest company in any market will win.

Who

This workout is for you if the following is familiar to you:

- Unknown time to market – you don't know how long it takes to get ideas into market.
- You are too slow to get into market.
- Bottlenecks – there are too many bottlenecks hindering progress.
- Dependencies – teams are tangled in a complex mess of dependencies.
- Not taking a customer-centric, E2E (end to end) approach to value-creating processes.
- You have silos instead of cross-functional collaboration.
- You are starting all operating model designs with a focus on a 'fixed' organisational structure.
- You spend not enough time looking at flow of work, cross-team collaboration and technology constraints.
- Local optimising of internal process is not delivering great value or outcomes.

What you will learn in this workout:

- Accelerate speed to market with FLOW and reduce bottlenecks.
- Flexible and adaptable organisational team design and structures.

Why

Market leader or market lagger?

As organisations grow bigger and more complex, it seems the more people there are the more impossible it is to get things done. Everyone is too busy. Accelerating time to value is essential to stay competitive.

To achieve this there are two key focus areas:

- business flow
- organisational structures.

How you get work done matters

How you get work done matters. This idea is a game changer and can mean the difference between top of game to market lagger. Good business flow describes an organisational system that's able to provide a consistent flow of value to its customers. Bad flow occurs when people work in functional silos and there are too many dependencies and handoffs that lead to organisational bottlenecks.

In this workout, I will show you how to solve this problem of speed in your organisation, which will enable you to increase profits by reducing organisational bottlenecks. There are five key benefits to what you will learn:

- **Become customer-centric:** Bet small before betting big by using quick feedback loops to prioritise.
- **Maximise profits:** Optimising flow will make it cheaper to meet customer needs.
- **Boost productivity:** Develop faster speed to market.
- **Improve agility:** Develop the ability to pivot and adapt to in-market changes with minimal cost impact.
- **Develop happier people:** Have less burnout and people working on the right things, not everything.

In this section, you will learn what business flow is and how to optimise it. I will provide you with some activities so you can learn by doing, while providing case studies to help you understand what good looks like and what to avoid.

What

For **A – Accelerate time to value** there are two focus areas:

- **Organisational structure:**
  - Set up an organisational structure designed for speed and adaptability. Think of it more like an living breathing ecosystem rather than a fixed mechanical system.
  - Understand an organisational structure is constantly changing, like a tree.
- **Business flow:**
  - Business flow is how work gets done in the organisation.
  - Best practice is orienting everyone to delivering value for the customer rather than silo work.

Where the wheels fall off

When organisations want to become agile, it seems to start in HR, which means it moves quickly to what 'hierarchy' needs to be put into place and what roles should be made redundant. This immediately changes the focus and energy of an agility rollout. Don't start there. There should be minimal to no dependencies on a system, process or other team's perspective.

Key principles to setting up an organisational structure

It is not just people, there are other factors:

- Flow of work – how value is delivered to the customer.
- People and mastery – encouraging best practices and enabling people to get better.
- Speed to market – designing an organisation for speed to market.
- Adaptability – creating a flexible, adaptive organisational structure than can handle changing priorities.
- Technology architecture – can be a constraint and needs to be a consideration in team set up.

Organisation structure is already in place?

Don't worry if this ship has sailed already. My favourite tactic is to create 'virtual' teams to work together. I actually prefer this method because it means your structure is flexible and adaptive and can change based on objectives and what needs to be achieved. Please don't restructure – it is demoralising for everyone and stops organisational uplift as people don't cope well with the uncertainty.

Long-lived teams are not a silver bullet

So many organisations *love* long-lived teams. Long-lived teams work best because it takes time for people to storm, form and build trust, and to understand the mission and how to achieve it. If this makes strategic sense to you and you have the money to support it, then go for it. However, there is a downside, which is it's *expensive* – the most common end state is a feature factory that produces features regardless of whether the customer wants or needs them. Most organisations cannot afford the luxury of long-lived teams, but you should understand the intent of them and adapt based on your own customer needs and budgetary requirements.

What is business flow?

To help you understand what business flow is and how it works, there are five new terms you need to learn:

1. Flow	· The set of activities needed to turn an idea into value in customers' hands.
	· The quicker and cheaper you can perform flow the more likely you can make a profit, stay competitive and survive.
	· Flow is split into 'lead time' and 'cycle time'.
	· It is critical to baseline flow and prove what you are doing is working.
2. Lead time	· The start of flow from idea to when the work or build is started.
	· It will include activities such as business case, request for proposal (RFP) and budget approvals.

3. Cycle time
- The time from when work is started until the value is in customers' hands.
- It will include software build, environments, testing and deployments.

4. Activity time
- Every task performed is simply called an 'activity'.
- You want to track how long each activity takes to complete.

5. Wait time
- In large organisations, hand-off of tasks is normal.
- When a task needs to be handed off to another team, it frequently involves waiting until the other team is ready to start it.

Okay – you now have enough information to get started on optimising your flow!

Tactics

Understanding business flow requires people to practise and understand it at a more simple level before trying to understand it at a more complex organisational level.

Learn by doing activity

Let's use a very simple example to explain how it works. You will then have the skills and language to apply in a more complex organisational example.

I will share my morning routine with you. Every morning, I get a coffee from the local coffee shop. I am not a morning person, as my partner will attest to – so I don't really wake up until after my coffee. I live inner city in self-declared coffee capital Melbourne. So I have a lot of choice of coffee shops, and making good coffee is definitely considered an art and a profession. As a consequence they take coffee very seriously, which means I always get a good coffee but it is expensive and it can take from five to fifteen minutes. Even though I really want a morning coffee, sometimes I don't bother if I am in a rush. So let's walk through how it works ...

I arrive at the coffee shop and there is a queue of people. I wait five minutes for my turn. When I get to the counter, I want to know what the muffin special of the day is. The server doesn't know and has to send a question back to the kitchen. It is macadamia, which I dislike so I only order coffee. I pay for my coffee and I sit on the stool by the barista. The barista calls name after name, and eventually my name is called. It has taken 15 minutes to get coffee.

Let's align some of our new language with this example – categorising my coffee run into work and wait times. What is longer, the activity time or the wait time? What are the bottlenecks? Are there alternate ways to achieve the same goal?

How would you optimise the coffee shop for speed to value? They could reduce wait times by:

- allowing me to look at the menu on my phone
- creating a mobile ability to order and pay
- having a menu on display at the front of the shop
- experimenting with one person preparing milk constantly and one on bean grinding to see if it is quicker.

Five key steps

There are five key steps that if followed will significantly reduce your time to market:

1. **Make flow visible:** The essential first step is to make the workflow, wait times and bottlenecks visible, with the time of each. This will change the narrative from opinion to fact based, and it will encourage people to look outside their functional silos.

2. **Reduce wait times:** It always comes as a surprise to people that the #1 productivity benefit is reducing or removing wait times. Baseline your flow, track your wait times and see if it is true in your organisation.

3. **WIP limits:** This is the power of doing less. The best analogy for this is a traffic jam. The more cars on the road, the longer it takes to get to your destination. The same applies to people and work. Learn how introducing work in progress (WIP) limits will enable smooth flow.

4. **Small batches:** True agility can only be achieved if you deliver value in small increments. Small batches will enable you to pivot and change your mind with minimal cost impact.

5. **Continuous learning:** The bottlenecks you face today and the bottlenecks you will face in 12 months will be different. Encourage people to keep the discussion and learning open.

Getting started – learn by doing activity

I have a tactic you can utilise to catch everyone's attention in 20 minutes and help them understand why this is important. Get your team into a room, have multiple tables with a bag of Lego on each. Tell everyone to find a table and start building using the Lego. Give them 10 minutes.

What will happen is that each table will work separately to build something. People naturally lean into silos. At the end of the exercise, inform them that at no time were they told to work separately. They simply choose to work that way themselves.

Then you inform them that if they had put their Lego together and worked as one team, they would have realised that all the pieces built a bridge.

This is a simple powerful game to encourage discussion on silos and cross-team collaboration.

Wins

- **Become customer-centric:** Bet small before betting big by using quick feedback loops to prioritise.
- **Maximise profits:** Optimise flow to make it cheaper to meet customer needs.
- **Boost productivity:** Develop faster speed to market.
- **Improve agility:** Develop the ability to pivot and adapt to in-market changes with minimal cost impact.
- **Develop happier people:** Have less burnout and people working on the right things, not everything.

Real-life case study – reduced wait times

Problem

I was engaged by a CFO in an energy utility company. The organisation was frustrated at how slow technology was. I was told this was the #1 bottleneck. The remit was to make them quicker by improving their delivery. This was a non-agile environment with a six-stage gate process.

Approach

I tracked 14 projects going through the different stage gates and baselined the data. The average time to market was two years. However, the lead time was 12 to 18 months and the cycle times were 6 to 12 months. Across the 14 projects, the largest time to complete was the business case stage. It was taking up to 12 months to get business cases approved. This was 80% due to wait times.

Observations

Finance had become a bottleneck as they insisted on reading, understanding, editing and providing opinions on all business cases in the organisation. So the real issue was that people were frustrated because getting to the work stage was so slow. The technology team were not set up for success.

Solution

We introduced two changes:

- business case lite, which had a six-week process
- dedicated funding streams for strategic initiatives preapproved as board-endorsed objectives.

This resulted in time to market reducing by over 50%.

Real-life case study – why executive sponsorship is critical

Problem

Any time you want things to be done differently, you need a circuit breaker. Frequently, the only person who can make this happen cross-functionally is a person with the authority to do so. Hierarchy matters in large organisations. This means executive leads must stand up and take a risk and lean into helping teams.

A junior member of a team was talking to the CIO at a large bank. They were casually chatting about a new release that needed to go live. The team couldn't make a launch date commitment because they were unsure on when they would get access to environments they needed. The CIO was surprised to hear this was an issue.

Approach

The CIO asked for the flow of work to be presented at the next technology leadership session. For the past six months, it had taken up to six weeks for teams to get a working environment to utilise for their work.

Observations

With the flow of work mapped out, it showed just six hours of work across six weeks elapsed time. The problem was the number of teams involved, all with their own priorities and work queues.

Solution

This issue had struggled to get traction for the prior six months; however, with executive sponsorship it was solved in three weeks. Without the CIO to champion the case, the change would not have occurred.

Way forward

Most CEOs want to increase the productivity of their organisation. So a lot of them love the benefits you will get with this workout. However, I have it as step 4 of 6 in this workout series. Increasing speed in the wrong direction is not beneficial at all. So, while this workout is powerful, take heed that before you increase speed, you must be pointing in the right direction.

So what workout is next? **C – Cadence, fast and frequent**. This workout is all about repeatability and consistency. Repeatability is key to ensuring you have good habits, and consistency is all about communication. It is unspoken communication; if you and your team know what is required when, and everyone just knows it without saying it, you can move in unison. This enables speed.

IMPACT– CADENCE, FAST AND FREQUENT

The whole is greater than the sum of the parts

Who

This workout is for you if the following is familiar to you:

- No organisational rhythm – your functional units decide on their own operating rhythm.
- Functional teams operate in functional silos.
- Change fatigue – your teams are struggling with never-ending change.
- Unplanned work is impacting progress of planned initiatives.

What you will learn in this workout:

- Consistent cadence will provide better communication and expectations of what and when.
- Cross-team collaboration will improve because everyone will be working on the same rhythm.
- Good habits – a consistent cadence is like building muscle memory for healthy habits.

- Efficiency – all functions working on the same cadence will uplift efficiency in your organisation.

Why

Your organisation must move in sync

Have you ever seen a flock of birds move in sync? Or a school of fish? It is stunning and mesmerising. This is an example of a complex adaptive system. To understand the power of the system, you don't focus on the smallest piece, the bird. The focus needs to be the flock, which is the collection of all the birds.

Organisations are also complex adaptive systems. The power of an organisation is unleashed not when each part of the organisation does its own thing but when each part has the ability to synchronise with each other part, just like a flock of birds.

Obviously, the more people you have in an organisation, the more complicated the communication and collaboration between those people is. This is where cadence is a critical component to success.

Unspoken communication for speed

Cadence simplifies communication and collaboration by giving everyone an understanding of when something is supposed to happen and how often. A repeatable cadence is immensely important to the effectiveness of an organisation. If everyone knows when something is meant to happen, it reduces the chaos and people can align to the agreed rhythm.

Spotting trends

Creating an organisational cadence is like building your organisational muscles for performance. The more repeatable your rhythm is, the less chaos and the greater the efficiency you will see in your teams. My favourite part of a cadence is that it allows you to pattern your organisation and what you have achieved, so you can spot trends and compare easily what is good and what is bad. It allows a greater association between root causes and outcomes, which is a great way to learn as an organisation.

Organisational pulse

Think of establishing a cadence for your organisation as the pulse of the organisation – like a drum, keeping the beat. It is steady and predictable; it sets the pace for everyone and keeps everyone aligned and working as a whole. Using cadence and rituals is like tapping into the energy of an organisation. Rituals strengthen team bonds and can help reinforce desired behaviours. They will enforce your organisation's identity and unity.

What

Cadence will help you turn words into action and operationalise what needs to be done

Cadence is routines, processes and systems occurring in a repeatable fashion. Cadence is the rhythm of your organisation. It keeps all teams in the organisation in sync. It is also the rhythm you use to deliver change. Cadence works when people, teams, objectives, performance, strategy, money and KPIs all align to the same pace.

The simplest cadence in an organisation is to align goals, plans and so on with the calendar and financial year:

- annual
- quarterly
- monthly
- weekly.

Not everyone likes this, but it is practical and aligns with tax, financial and regulatory external timelines.

The missing ingredient

Where organisations go wrong is that this cadence is not just a moment in time. The intent of the cadence is to *finish* something in the slotted time so that you can pivot to something else if required. It is not about simply finishing a milestone. *Finish* means that you have pushed something into market and are ready to accept feedback on user behaviour to see if what you delivered added the assumed behaviour.

Tactics

Getting started

So, how to set up your organisational cadence? The optimal approach is to start quarterly:

- OKRs – identify what can be achieved in the quarter (this means *finished*).
- Strategic alignment – map the quarterly OKRs to your north star.
- Batches – break work down into small batches that can be done in a quarter.
- Work – map work *and* capacity to OKRs; there must be 100% alignment.

Sounds simple, right? Actually it is not and it requires discipline and transparency and time to embed.

Planned work versus unplanned work

- The above is considered planned work – what happens is unplanned work often interrupts it.
- Track unplanned work to find out why it is not planned.
- It takes teams a little bit of time and discipline to identify what they can achieve.

HOW is not the focus

- The above does not focus on HOW; HOW is the team's choice.
- The people doing the work are best placed to decide how to optimise it.
- External assistance is in the form of WHY and measures.

Predictability

So many organisations work on a quarterly rhythm, but no one ever checks a team's ability to 'say what you do' and 'do what you say'. In my experience, upfront the team will have less than a 50% ability to predict their work for 12 weeks. The goal is to track, and learn from the measure, what is causing them problems.

Conflicting OKRs

Lots of organisations do not set their team structures up properly. To achieve their quarterly objectives, they need assistance from another team. However, that team has a full set of objectives and a full book of work so can't help. Frequently they don't declare this upfront and state they will 'try their best'.

Track dependencies to ensure teams have capacity to complete them.

Wins

- Improved collaboration across functional units.
- Controlled change rather than chaotic change.
- The ability to learn, track and observe across repeatable cadences.
- Breaking work into small drops of value, enabling the ability to pivot and create true agility.

Examples

Example 1 – No enterprise rhythm

Organisations that do not have an enterprise rhythm are less efficient and less harmonious cross-functionally. For example, IT is working on a big release so are overworked and burnt out, yet HR decide they want everyone to go on leadership training and assume August is a good month to do it. The optimal approach would be all work for the month or quarter would be put into the system to make it visible. It would be prioritised against objectives and OKRs and then there would be no surprises and teams can negotiate on what works to create happy teams.

Example 2 – Enterprise rhythm but does not apply to all teams

This example is very similar to the first example. What happens is you get teams to work on a quarterly cycle. They spend a week working on their priorities for the quarter and present them back, get approval and start the quarter. Within one week of the quarter starting, work comes in from other functions; for example, finance wants to run an audit or HR wants to run feedback sessions. All of this takes time.

I frequently use planned versus unplanned work to make this problem visible. I track it. I make it visible. I bring it into discussions so people understand the impact on the quarterly outcome.

Way forward

Use this workout to introduce an organisational pulse for good habits:

- Start of cadence – baseline and say what you will do.
- Track progress – use metrics and evidence from baseline.
- End of cadence – track predictability.
- Reflection – did this cadence move us closer to the north star? If not, pivot.

Okay, the last workout to have a superstrong Outcomes muscle group is **T – Transparency**. This is all about transparency, governance and compliance.

IMPACT– TRANSPARENCY

Never run away from problems or pretend you don't notice them

Who

Frequently everything in organisations is assessed as going great, but the organisation is not any closer to their north star. Why? This happens when executives cannot accept the truth and instead lean into confirmation bias and skewed lenses and narratives. You simply will not achieve success without changing the dial to transparency instead of opinions and skewed lenses.

This workout is for you if the following is familiar to you:

- Toxic culture – sidebar discussions in splintered groups is how decisions are made.
- Conflicting opinions – different, conflicting opinions on progress.
- Executives and the team see different things.
- Lack of confidence on what the real problem is and how to tackle it.

- Progress – everything is 'green', but the organisation is going nowhere fast.
- No visibility into work queues, progress and bottlenecks.

What you will learn in this workout:

- How to move away from paper status 'watermelon' reporting (red inside, green outside).
- How to ensure as CEO you have access to what is going on 'on the ground'.
- How to get access to evidence quickly for speed of decisioning.
- How to introduce lean, federated governance across the entire organisation.

Why

Watermelon projects

Transparency is one of the cornerstones of agility. One of the norms in many organisations today is the concept of 'watermelon' projects. What's a watermelon project, I hear you ask? Well, if you take a good look at a watermelon, what colour is it on the inside and on the outside? That's right, it is green on the outside and red on the inside. So, who has worked on a project that has tracked green until the very last stage and then it tracks red? I know I have, a few times. A watermelon project is lacking transparency.

Stopping projects too late

It was in the news recently that an Australian bank had stopped a core project after spending $90M. Ouch. Another project bites the dust. Unfortunately, it is a common occurrence. So why did it take a spend of $90M to decide what they were doing was not going to work? I can almost guarantee you that the team on the ground knew this at least 12 months ahead of the executive team.

The blame game

So why does it happen and can you do anything to prevent it? Flagging a project as red means you will receive a lot of unwarranted scrutiny, attention and pressure, most of which is unhelpful in solving the problem. Hence, there is a reluctance from people to draw attention to their project, specifically at a time when they are desperately trying to do everything they can to bring it under control. However, at the same time, the people financing the project have a right to know how things are going. These conflicting situations can leave a team in a pickle.

What

Radical transparency is the deliberate and frequent sharing of information across teams and people. It increases openness about progress and process and helps to truly identify where you are at (situational awareness), which is critical for deciding on the right path forward and next steps. Here are some guidelines to getting it right:

- Mutual agreement – people must buy into transparency rather than it being imposed.
- Boundaries – have clear limits on what is suitable for transparency and what isn't; for example, certain information may be commercially or personally sensitive.
- Ethical use of transparency – with transparency comes a high-trust model; a team being open and transparent and having what they shared used against them will make it fail.

- Remove secrecy – toxic cultures use secrets and information as power.
- Everyone must be looking at the same data, with no wordsmithing.
- Understand data is not the destination but the start of your journey.
- Move away from vague conversations such as, 'Are you making progress?'
- Acknowledge that people may be resistant to being data driven.

Tactics

So for **T – Transparency** there are four tactics I recommend:

- common language
- evidence-based decisions
- visualisation
- governance alignment.

Common language + evidence = the secret ingredient for transparency at scale

Different teams speak different languages and lingo – you need to be able to introduce the concept of speaking the same language across different teams. You need this because you want to be able to compare and assess what is going well and what is not going well.

Examples include:

- **Organisational data categorisation and groupings:**
  - You need each team to categorise the same way (by product? by service?).
  - Financial data, sales data and technology data need to align to these categories.
  - You need separate 'run' activities and 'change' activities.

- **Tracking periods across all functions:**
  - Pick the same periods across the organisation.
  - You need to be able to see costs, value, done/not done across the same periods.
  - You need this to spot trends, such as which time period had higher performance.

- **Objectives and KPIs:**
  - You need all objectives to ladder from top to bottom and vice versa.
  - Each functional unit needs alignment.

- **Volume of work, effort, sizing:**
  - You need teams to break work down consistently into same-sized 'blocks'.
  - Effort/time tracking consistency across teams is critical – you want to use it to learn what is taking time and how much effort things take.

A common language is about creating patterns, a language taxonomy, so the data can be understood at enterprise level. This is a *game changer*. You will be able to see and understand the enterprise system of work and get the team to tell you what they are working on and how they are progressing with no middle person or wordsmithing. For the first time, a common language will give executives access to the same data as teams in a useful way that allows them to make decisions. This will give you speed of decisioning.

Visualisation

Many years ago, if I wanted to visualise data or a system of work, I would need to ask for IT's help, but today with tools such as PowerBI and Thoughtspot, visualisation can be implemented quickly and powerfully, and you can see the system of work like never before. The old world is status reporting that is a few weeks out of date; the new world is real-time dashboards based on data input by the team. The executive team can now access accurate real-time data to make decisions quickly.

Governance

I am unsure why, but many people do not think governance is relevant for agility. This is illogical. Governance is always applicable. The only question on the table is how it is done. Governance should be about due diligence and enabling teams, not slowing them down. The best approach to governance is federated decision-making. Put the decision-making with the work and give teams guardrails and create transparency.

With a common language, visualisation into the work being performed, using data and not opinions, and the same cadence for all teams, you have all the ingredients for a successful governance framework. The missing piece is financial, which you should be able to align with cadence – usually quarterly – so you can see how much a quarter has cost, what value was delivered to customers' hands, what work was completed and what metrics were positively or negatively impacted.

The governance team now has everything for 100% alignment and traceability, and it can help highlight gaps to help teams understand where they should focus for success.

Wins

- **Speed of decisioning:** Teams and executives using the same data in real time.
- **Accuracy:** Accurate data on current state of play, meaning good decisions can be made.
- **Enterprise transparency:** A 360-degree view of what people are working on and the relevant figures.
- **Systematic:** Structured approach to enterprise working as a whole.
- **Trust:** Sharing information is a great motivator and provides psychological safety.
- **Culture uplift:** When everyone can access the same data, there will be an inability to use information as power.
- **Empowered teams:** Educating people on the impact of actions on results.
- **Alignment:** Having everyone use a single source of truth ensures clarity and alignment.

Real-life case study – a toxic culture

I was in a meeting room a few years ago with a number of executive leaders when a peer of mine presented some inaccurate, misleading and negative financial numbers about something my team was working on. The information was so completely wrong, and I was so surprised by what was presented, that I assumed I had misheard. I validated that this position was inaccurate and I provided the real data; however, the damage was done. It would seem that my peer had shared this data far and wide before this session to ensure everyone 'understood' it. I assumed she had just made a mistake and I sat down with her to provide the accurate data. It was when she had no interest in the real data that I realised she didn't care and it had been done on purpose to undermine me in a public setting, knowing full well that I would be on the back foot and arguing too strongly would make me look defensive. Welcome to politics and toxic cultures in the corporate world, using misinformation as power.

Way forward

Direct observation is essential and no combination of indirect methods, however clever, can possibly take its place

Transparency over 'skewed' opinions

This transparency workout is the last workout required to make your Outcomes organisational muscles strong. Moving away from opinions and stale, out-of-date progress reporting will uplift the speed of decisioning in your organisation. It will also give you access to what is actually going on in your organisation rather than relying on a skewed perspective that one person wishes to paint so they are viewed in a more favourable light.

Everyone has access to the same data

A lot of large successful organisations have championed transparency as the reason for their success. Jack Stack, CEO of SRC Holdings and creator of The Great Game of Business, opened up the company's books and taught employees the impact of their actions on the company financials. When the employees had access to the data, Stack found they were able to engage in intelligent and forward-looking decisions about margins and profits.

One source of truth

Transparency is the starting position to changing your culture. Everyone needs access to a single source of truth. We all must speak in a common, easy-to-understand language regardless of whether we are the CFO, a developer, a technology architect or the marketing team. When we utilise data over opinion and everyone has access to the same data, we will unleash the power of everyone in the organisation. The fact that most organisations today are run on paper reports based on opinions one step removed from the data doesn't make sense in the digital age.

YOUR OUTCOMES MUSCLE GROUP IS NOW FITTER AND STRONGER

Be outcome focused

Okay, you did it! Six workouts designed to make your Outcomes muscles stronger! Each workout is designed to solve a specific organisational problem.

Organisations that have a strong Outcomes muscle group understand how they deliver value to their customers and why their customers choose them over their competitors. All functions and teams are pointing in the same direction and working on the agreed priorities of the customers, while achieving ROI and exploring potential new customers and needs.

These workouts will make you stronger and fitter as an organisation. They are designed to be utilised discretely or as a set of workouts done at the same time. Both approaches work; it just depends on your organisational need.

BEHAVIOURS CHANGE CULTURES

The next muscle group is Behaviours. Organisations frequently want to change their way of working by focusing on processes. However, unless people change their behaviours, the change will not stick. People learn bad habits and behaviours, and eventually it just becomes the organisational culture and DNA. Culture is a lag indicator and behaviour is a lead indicator. Impacting lead indicators will have a direct effect on lag indicators.

In the next chapter, we examine changing toxic or poor-performing cultures into high-performance teams and people. To do that, we need to lean into the five dysfunctions of teams, understand what they are and what workouts will change them!

CHAPTER 7
<u>HOW</u> – BEHAVIOURAL-LED CULTURE

COMPANIES NEED TO GET
AWAY FROM INGRAINED
DYSFUNCTIONAL BEHAVIOURS
ACROSS THE BOARD TO ACHIEVE
LASTING TRANSFORMATION

WHY WE NEED TO CHANGE BEHAVIOURS

Fast and adaptive organisations have different people behaviour and characteristics

If you wish to transform your organisation into a fast and adaptive organisation, you must alter people's behaviour for the change to take root, seed and grow. Organisations are slow and bureaucratic when only a small number of people hold all the power, because it is impossible to move at pace with only a few decision-makers. The behaviours that are successful in a slow and bureaucratic organisation are obviously different compared to a fast and adaptive organisation. To transform your organisation, you must take a good look at who benefits from a slow and bureaucratic organisation, because these will be the people who will white-ant the new way of working. The best way to deal with this situation is to change your incentive and reward structures to incentivise the behaviours you want. Simply do not ignore it. You must get ahead of this to have any impact or to ensure that the change sticks in your organisation.

Culture is a lag indicator, behaviour is a lead indicator

Culture is king. Rolling out a new way of working without unpicking your current culture won't work.

New ways of working require people to change how they work to accept them. This is especially important in siloed organisations where hierarchy is power. People need to unlearn bad behaviours and learn new behaviours that benefit everyone as opposed to the selected few.

However, culture is a hard thing to quantify and create. Culture is a lag indicator. To improve a culture, we need to focus on lead indicators. The lead indictors for a good culture are people behaviours. If you work on improving and uplifting the lead indicators, the culture uplift will happen naturally.

The unspoken truth

'The great resignation' is a term coined by organisational psychologist Anthony Klotz and is one of the latest trending topics debated frequently in the media. The original trigger was the COVID pandemic, which caused people to question why they were spending so much time doing something that did not make them happy.

The #1 reason people are quitting their jobs is toxic culture.[31] Yet, when you work in a corporate environment, the concept of toxic culture is not discussed or mentioned, ever. Most people working in an unhealthy culture fear speaking out because the consequences can be terrifying. Speak up and you will get picked on next or lose your job.

Culture is the key issue standing in the way of converting your organisation to true agility. Agility requires the status quo to change, and yet you have so many people who benefit from the status quo who do not want it to change. Large organisations breed mini fiefdoms and power struggles, and unfortunately bad behaviour is contagious and people inflict damage – mostly covertly or passive aggressively – on others because they feel it is critical for self-preservation. It seems everyone is playing a zero-sum game.

Zero-sum game

A situation in which one person or group can win only by causing another person or group to lose. Sound familiar? Corporate environments need to be win–win to change culture and deliver any successful transformation. Agility requires you to unleash the power of *everyone* in the organisation, not just the ones holding the power and political strings. No one seems to think they are part of the problem, yet this is not possible.

For culture to change it requires people with good heart and good intent to stand up for those who are not empowered. Are you willing to play this role? Someone must. You don't need to do it alone, but it needs to be done for lasting change.

The dysfunctions of a team

The Five Dysfunctions of a Team by Patrick Lencioni is a great book on what *not* to do. The five dysfunctions defined by Lencioni are:

- **Absence of trust:** Not validating what you hear; lack of empathy; thinking you know better.

- **Fear of conflict:** Seeking artificial harmony; encouraging silence over constructive dialogue.
- **Lack of commitment:** Pretending there is buy-in for certain group decisions.
- **Avoidance of accountability:** Counterproductive behaviour encouraging division over unity.
- **Inattention to results:** Allowing people to focus on personal status and ego over getting desired results.

So where does culture go off the rails?

Like most things, it's actually hard to spot. When you look at the surface, everything looks fine, but it is simply a thin veneer and everyone knows the environment is not safe. However, in my experience there are some simple behaviours that if they are stopped and replaced with positive behaviours the rewards are large.

I have many years' experience in leading large and small teams, and toxic cultures start with the leader. That's you and me. This is really worth thinking about; are you a toxic leader? Most people will say no, but quite a lot of people don't realise they are. The people in your teams will simply follow your example. Most people seem to think that because they have friends at work or the people who report to them are nice that there are no issues. This is not a good way to measure success.

Warning bells

Stuff to watch for that may not be obvious on first glance:

- **Gossip** – talking about people behind their backs.
- **Gaslighting** – be very careful about listening to what people say about others. A lot of people have an agenda that will always be in their own favour. It is very common for people to twist stories to paint someone in a positive or a negative light to get a personal win. Don't allow such manipulation. Go directly to the source and validate or discuss in an open forum. If you do this, people are less likely to manipulate the information they give you because there are no wins for them.

- **Cronies**[32] – people who are hired or promoted but generally lack the skill, experience or qualifications for the job. Cronies grant each other positions, favours and benefits. Those who lack skills are the ones most likely to never challenge their boss. Loyalty is favoured above capability, and keeping the existing fiefdom in power is the main goal, not business results. People who surround themselves with cronies do not want the status quo to change. They will keep highly capable people off the radar, forcing them to leave your organisation unless they agree to blind loyalty.

- **Groupthink** – closely aligns with cronies. You will not get a good organisational outcome if everyone agrees with each other. Healthy conflict is a positive.

- **Bullies** – such a misunderstood bunch. People think bullies are ogres with warts on their noses and are easy to spot, but they are not. I don't know anyone in the workplace who thinks they are a bully themselves but, again, this simply cannot be true.

The bottom line is that people get away with their behaviour mostly because of the company and the culture it fosters. We want to look at the personalities of the perpetrators and say, well, that explains it. No, it doesn't. What really explains it is the work environment that provided the opportunities. It allowed these people to get hired in the first place and then to operate with impunity.

Leaders must go first

Behavioural change starts at the top. It is usually the leadership group that needs to change first for the organisational transformation to have any chance of success. Leaders must role model the changes and behaviours. This is required to set the tone for the rest of the organisation on what the new definition of 'good' is.

So if you wish to transform your organisation into fast and adaptive, behavioural change is a non-negotiable. Behavioural change simply won't happen by itself. You must foster it.

A happy workforce is a more productive workforce

A high-performing organisation is an organisation where people feel value and fulfilled. We spend so much of our time at work; for it not to be enjoyable is soul destroying.

While it is possible to get business success without looking after your workforce, in my experience, leaders who care only about the bottom line are short-term focused and are not getting the best outcome for the organisation longer term. Hiring and training to get people up to speed is time and dollar intensive. So, if you want to future-proof your organisation and unleash the power of enterprise agility, look after your #1 asset: your people.

A motivated workforce is much more productive. Numerous studies have shown this:

- Oxford University ran a study that found a happy workforce is 13% more productive.[33]
- Forbes highlighted a similar study that came up with the figure of 20% more productive.[34]
- Inc. noted many benefits of a happy workforce, including that innovation flourished.[35]

A happy workplace is usually a productive, flexible and resilient workplace.

WORKOUTS TO BUILD YOUR BEHAVIOURS AGILITY MUSCLE GROUP

Let's get started

In this chapter, there is a series of workouts designed to change team behaviours and ultimately culture, which I call FACES. This approach is about grassroots ownership of behavioural change. It is a structured method for changing behaviours. It identifies what problems you have and the best way to solve them. There are five workouts in total.

Problem to be solved	How to solve it	Why it solves it
Gossiping, rumours, factions	**F** – Make FEEDBACK normal	Feedback is discussed in open forums not behind closed doors. Encourages people to share their concerns directly.
Groupthink	**A** – ACCOUNTABILITY with radical candour	If you want to change the status quo, you need to encourage honesty and discussion on what is wrong.
Unresolved conflict Lack of respect among team members	**C** – healthy CONFLICT management	Teach people how to fight fairly. Agree on ground rules for decision-making. Create awareness that not all decisions will go your way but we accept them and agree to support them.
Creating awareness of how your behaviour impacts the group	**E** – ENERGY multipliers and drainers	Teaches the team to understand what ingredients give the right conditions for high performance and what makes the team work suboptimally.
Getting people to focus on improving themselves and what they bring to the table	**S** – SELF-AWARENESS	Teaches people we all have strengths and weaknesses and we can't control others but we can control and uplift our character muscles.

Going for gold

- Custom-design your agility journey by picking which workouts will deliver quick wins.
- Baseline your starting position with evidence and metrics.
- Reflect every six weeks; what has made a difference?
- Adapt, rerun and embed what's working well.

FACES – MAKE FEEDBACK NORMAL

Who

This workout is for you if the following are familiar to you:

- Gossip and factions are the norm.
- Feedback is not a frequent occurrence with your team.
- You assume what is going on, rather than asking directly.
- You ask people not directly affected and involved.
- Feedback is frequently not well received or is delivered badly.
- Feedback is not welcomed or encouraged.
- Feedback is for annual performance not improvement.
- Blame and feedback are often confused.
- Constructive criticism and feedback are assumed to be the same thing.

What you will learn in this workout:

- What good feedback is and how to provide it and receive it.
- Tactics to embed a feedback culture in your teams.
- The benefits of feedback in breaking down toxic cultures.
- How to utilise feedback to drive continuous improvement.

Why

A healthy culture starts with stopping bad behaviours such as gossiping, bullying and backstabbing. This behaviour is stopped by encouraging a safe environment and ensuring feedback is provided in an open environment. Team members should not share their feedback about others without the person in the room. Teaching your team to do this will have a really big impact on trust; if you bring in an open dialogue rule, people will trust each other more because they will not have to worry about backstabbing.

In most organisations, HR would have you believe that feedback is a normal state of play. They will run monthly employee surveys and share the insights from the survey on what needs to improve. However, real feedback is between people; it is not delivered via surveys. It is something a team needs to own themselves to really learn from it. Feedback is a journey. If your team has never done feedback before, you cannot deep dive into direct feedback immediately – they will run for the hills. You need to start gently, create awareness of the problem and what you are trying to achieve, educate people on what good and bad is, and then ask them to give it a go before judging it.

Do not assume people know how to give feedback or even understand what it is. Most don't. Go back to basics and start everyone at the start. Your team will resist starting a feedback culture because they are worried about what will be shared with them or they are worried about sharing their feelings. You need to help them move past this stage.

Benefits of a feedback culture include:

- **Growth and improvement:** There will be no growth or team improvement without feedback.
- **Increased trust:** Providing quality feedback will increase trust among your team.
- **Reduced gossip:** A feedback culture reduces gossip.

Mistaken assumptions about feedback include:

- It is about sharing your opinion on what someone has done.
- It is all about areas of improvement rather than acknowledgement of what worked.
- There is nothing to learn from the process and it's a waste of time and energy.
- It is about performance and not improvement.

Getting started

The biggest blocker to a feedback culture is lack of psychological safety. Do not assume it is not an issue in your team simply because it is not an issue for you. I have yet to meet a team where safety is not a concern.

The next blocker is helping people understand why feedback is provided – to help others learn and grow. This context must be constantly revisited. Too frequently feedback moves into opinion and 'you need to do it my way'.

What

What is feedback?

Ultimately, feedback is about communication. You need feedback to learn and grow. Receiving feedback can be a stressful experience. That's why many people hesitate to ask for it. But the more often you do, the less stressful it becomes to initiate the conversation and to hear the comments. Giving feedback is a skill. And like all skills, it takes practice to get it right. There are lots of different types of feedback. I recommend focusing your energies on two types:

- Appreciation feedback – acknowledgement of what has added value this week.
- Forward feedback – feedback to use in future scenarios for success.

Tactics

So for **F – Make feedback normal**, there are two tactics I recommend: social charters and feedforward.

Social charters

This is when a social contract gets discussed and written up where everyone agrees what kind of environment you want to foster. Talk about:

- Gossip and talking behind people's backs – discuss how this impacts the team.
- Mutual accountability – not listening to or providing gossip.

- Decency – if you have something to say to someone, you say it directly to them.
- Honour – you don't get to provide feedback unless you work with someone.

Write it up in a social contract. Everyone signs it. Then discuss it monthly: do we honour it? Is it ignored?

Feedforward

Most of the feedback we receive isn't actually very useful. It's often filled with platitudes and vague labels like 'inspiring', 'great' or 'lacking executive presence'. To provide good feedback actually requires some effort and thought. I have tried and tested many feedback strategies, but the simplest and most effective is feedforward.

Feedback focuses on the past. *Feedforward* focuses on the future. For example, I recently gave a presentation to a group of 30 senior stakeholders. I asked my manager if he felt the session went well and if they had any feedback for me. He told me the presentation went well.

He also suggested when running a similar session in the future to perhaps ask more questions to the audience to allow them to engage with the content more and to understand their current perspectives. He then offered to role play and practise with me so I could learn to incorporate more questioning.

This is feedforward, focusing on the future rather than the past. Instead of critiquing, the focus is on enabling and helping. People are less likely to take this feedback personally and to become defensive.

Learn by doing activity – feedforward speed–dating style

- Scheduled monthly – not ad-hoc.
- Mandatory for everyone, including CEO.
- 90-minute activity for eight people who work with each other:
  - 30 minutes prep work/write feedforward cards
  - 60 minutes speed feedforward.
- Four tables with two people on each table.
- One person moves every six minutes. One person stays at the table.

- Everyone has three feedforward cards per person.
- Answer three questions per person:
  - List one (or more if desired) accomplishment you really appreciated from this individual the previous month that you'd like to see more of, from either a business or culture point of view.
  - List one (or more if desired) challenge you'd like this individual to focus on next month, from either a business or culture point of view.
  - Is there anything else you'd like to let this individual know about their performance of their day-to-day tasks and overall contribution from this past month?
- Take turns talking through the cards; leave the cards with the person.
- On completion, discuss commonality between cards and what they learnt and how they will apply it.

Wins

- **Fun:** Speed feedforward run monthly in my experience ends up being a fun activity.
- **Healthy outlet for opinions:** People are encouraged to tackle issues in a useful and positive way.
- **Promotes decency:** People are encouraged to raise feedback directly and intent stays honourable.
- **Holds people accountable:** Feedforward cards are held by the recipient for future reflection and accountability.
- **Useful:** Feedforward rather than feedback helps make it useable in future situations.

Way forward

This workout is designed to get everyone comfortable with giving and receiving feedback. So many people dislike feedback because it is not done frequently enough. If we start to increase the frequency of the feedback, we make it normal and people start to uplift their skill in providing feedback. This is the critical path forward so that resentment doesn't build and you encourage people to lean into appreciation as well as critical feedback.

The next workout that we come to is **A – Accountability with radical candour**. So many people in organisations are fearful of sharing what they think. Silence ends up being golden and what happens is people check out and say nothing. If you want an engaged group of people in your organisation, you need to give them psychological safety to share their honest opinions without retribution, and you need to provide mechanics for resolving differences of opinions in a way that is respected by all. We need everyone to align behind decisions and not white-ant decisions behind the scenes.

FACES – ACCOUNTABILITY WITH RADICAL CANDOUR

Who

This workout is for you if the following is familiar to you:

- Command and control is the current method of management.
- People are not encouraged to challenge, discuss or debate.
- People are penalised for disagreeing with the leader's opinion.
- People say one thing in meetings and another thing outside meetings.
- People are hearing but not listening to other team members.

What you will learn in this workout:

- How to encourage people to tell it like it is.
- How to accept a difference of opinion and move forward.
- How to get real alignment and cohesion across a team.
- How to challenge directly but with kindness and care.

Why

Psychological safety is a precondition for any high-performance team. To achieve it, you need to encourage your team to be honest and direct while being kind and ethical. It takes time for people to learn the language and words to do this, and practice is key to getting it right to build the muscle. Candour is critical to building trust in your organisation. It is only when people speak their mind honestly and with integrity that people trust each other. Radical candour is a healthy mix of genuine praise and constructive criticism delivered kindly and respectfully. Radical candour is all about accountability to the team, the results and performance.

Kim Scott wrote a great book called *Radical Candour* and produced a framework (shown below) that is useful for organisations to refer to, and that should be front of mind and discussed on a frequent basis.

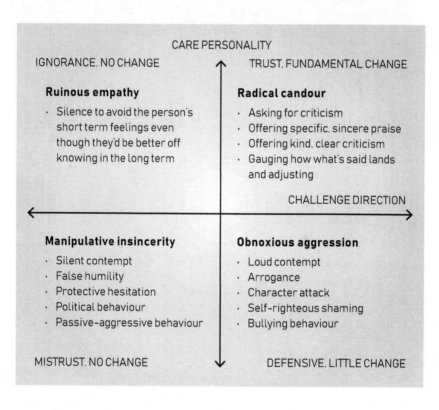

CARE PERSONALITY

IGNORANCE, NO CHANGE | TRUST, FUNDAMENTAL CHANGE

Ruinous empathy
- Silence to avoid the person's short term feelings even though they'd be better off knowing in the long term

Radical candour
- Asking for criticism
- Offering specific, sincere praise
- Offering kind, clear criticism
- Gauging how what's said lands and adjusting

CHALLENGE DIRECTION

Manipulative insincerity
- Silent contempt
- False humility
- Protective hesitation
- Political behaviour
- Passive-aggressive behaviour

Obnoxious aggression
- Loud contempt
- Arrogance
- Character attack
- Self-righteous shaming
- Bullying behaviour

MISTRUST, NO CHANGE | DEFENSIVE, LITTLE CHANGE

Most leaders struggle to deliver hard messages.[36] Global research from Edelman's Trust Barometer reveals that integrity is considered the #1 most desirable leadership quality. However, unfortunately only about 25% of people think their bosses actually have it. Honest feedback is the atomic building block of good management. There is nothing more damaging to human relationships than an imbalance of power. Candour is the honest broker of truth that neutralises the imbalance. The workplace is yearning for candid bosses, yet bosses continue to fall short. This is where radical candour comes in. It is a type of informal accountability because it will create positive outcomes and will create a culture of growth and pushing through comfort zones. It will encourage the development of you and your team members by offering guidance for ways that everyone can improve and be aware of what is adding value and what isn't adding value.

Radical candour and radical accountability are intrinsically linked, and both are linked to vulnerability. Radical accountability leads to saying what you do and doing what you say. To achieve it, you need radical candour about yourself and your actions, and when you fall short you need to own up to it.

What

So how do you build radical candour and radical accountability into your teams?

Radical candour

- Self-awareness – leaders go first:
  - Frequently refer to the provided radical candour framework.
  - Assess what your most natural style is and provide examples.
  - Talk through what action you have taken to improve.
- Share your stories – be vulnerable on when you did and didn't practise radical candour.
- Solicit feedback – prove you can take it before you start giving it out.
- Growth management – encourage one-on-one conversations for positive, direct and kind feedback, with examples.
- Never use other people's stories – they are not yours to share.
- Encourage people to share everything directly – encourage bravery.
- Give guidance, praise and criticism – but make sure to focus on the good stuff.

Build the preceding points into a repeatable rhythm; every fortnight is ideal but monthly at a minimum. Encourage baselining with the previous conversation and playback to stay anchored and to ensure the same message is not repeated over and over to show acknowledgement and improvement.

Radical accountability

- **Say/do ratio.** Are you accountable? Everyone will say yes, but how high is your say/do ratio? It is an interesting discussion. Can you prove it? Ask anyone if they are accountable – 100% of people will say yes ☺.

  Ask the question a different way: what evidence do they have that their say/do ratio is 100%? This applies as equally in your personal life as it does to your work life. What you say can be too vague and not understood by others.

- **Clear, concise communication.** Clear, concise communication is critical. Radical accountability drives optimal performance. When you allow others to take control of a specific situation you are giving up accountability.

  For example, say you blame one of your team members for not getting back to you about a report, but you did not specifically ask that person to do so. It's common to fail to recognise your role in misunderstandings. It's important you eliminate a victim and blame mentality. So clear, concise communication is critical for radical accountability and candour. The best way to achieve this is to develop healthy communication habits, especially around requests and promises.

- **Active listening.** Be aware that you cannot rate your own communication habits, only others can. Solicit feedback and utilise active listening where you encourage the other person to describe in their own words what they think the request is and how they will fulfil it. Good communication is a two-way loop not a one-way engagement. You cannot assume the message has been delivered successfully. You must validate with actions and words.

Way forward

A – Accountability with radical candour as a workout is about providing psychological safety to share honest opinions without repercussions, and that usually means you need to create space for uncomfortable honesty. Only with open dialogue can you move the dial. You cannot stop people feeling and thinking a certain way, so they may as well share it with an open group so you can deal with it in a constructive fashion, as opposed to it coming out in bad behaviours.

We are two workouts in out of five workouts that will turn your teams and people into a highly cohesive group. We started with feedback and accountability.

These workouts will bring conflict to the surface. That's okay. Conflict is not a bad thing; in fact, it is critical for creative tension and making ideas better. It is how you 'do' conflict that is the issue. The next workout is all about teaching people how to have healthy conflict.

FACES – HEALTHY CONFLICT MANAGEMENT

Who

This workout is for you if the following is familiar to you:

- Relationships – people not getting on with each other is distracting the focus of the team.
- Conflict style – the current mode of conflict management is passive aggression.
- Overwhelmed – people are aware of the impact but are unsure how to solve it.
- Factions – divisions have formed in your group rather than cohesion.

What you will learn in this workout:

- Impact – the negative impact of not dealing with conflict.
- Relationship strength – how conflict can increase trust within your team.
- Awareness – the pinch-crunch model and the implications of letting small things slide.

- How to face conflict – not seeking artificial harmony or encouraging silence over constructive dialogue.

Why

There is no such thing as a conflict-free environment. Not only that, but conflict is also good for teams. The only environments where conflict does not exist is in teams where there is no psychology safety, or there is groupthink. Conflict allows a team to come to terms with difficult situations, to synthesise diverse perspectives, and to make sure solutions are well thought out. In my experience, the best ideas or plans get better if pulled apart and reconstructed by a group. So we need healthy conflict in the workplace!*

Conflict is a normal part of life. When we don't share our opinions in a group, our opinions tend to come out behind closed doors to people one on one or as gossip because we did not agree with someone but refused to tell them, which is really not a healthy team dynamic.

It is inevitable that people on teams will find themselves in conflict, or at the very least annoyed or frustrated with each other. This is normal, and happens even in great teams. The difference between a good team and a great team is not in the amount of conflict, but in the way it is handled.

What

This workout for healthy conflict is based around two key concepts:

- the pinch-crunch model
- crucial conversations.

The pinch-crunch model

The basis of the pinch-crunch model of conflict management is that conflict can be predicted and reduced. Unresolved conflict affects production, lowers performance and fosters resentment. When expectations between

---

* For more on this, this *HBR* article sums it up well. Diversity requires enabling multiple perspectives, and when you manage to disagree ethically, you actually end up with greater trust and respect from people. https://hbr.org/2018/01/why-we-should-be-disagreeing-more-at-work.

people are not met, this creates a pinch or a breakdown in the existing relationship.

The pinch-crunch model helps us understand the importance of tackling minor issues (pinches) before they become major conflicts (crunches). If you address the pinch skilfully, it can be resolved in the moment without lasting impact. When minor issues are ignored and repeated over time, they can develop into a crunch. Once it becomes a crunch, it takes a lot more skill and effort to address it.

At the core, pinches are disruptions of our expectations. Usually, the other party has no idea that they have caused the rift that has you seething – 90% of difficult conversations can be traced back to an easy conversation that should have happened but didn't.

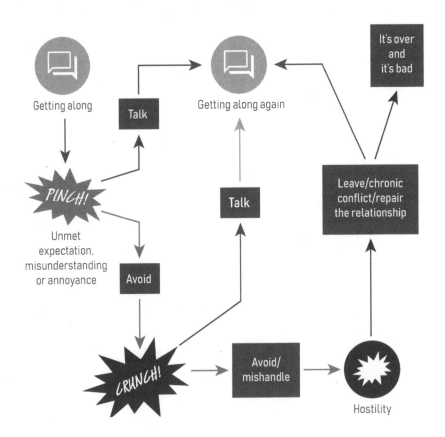

Here's how to implement the pinch-crunch model in your business:

Start the conversation	Watch this pinch-crunch video: https://www.youtube.com/watch?app=desktop&v=blIFtZ9E3oE Discuss moments of pinch that turned into a crunch in your workplace.
Self-awareness	Perform this activity to learn your own conflict style: https://transitionnetwork.org/wp-content/uploads/2021/08/6-Activity-Conflict-Styles.pdf?pdf=activity-conflict-styles This provides the group with language for future discussions.
Group discussion	Discuss as a group your own 'primary' conflict style and examples of how it manifests in work. It is important to not judge. Understand different styles may be required, dependent on context.
Building healthy conflict muscles	Do these two activities: · In weekly team meetings, ask people to share moments of pinch and crunch so you can normalise these discussions. · Create a team charter containing ground rules for conflict. These help teams build muscles for having stressful discussions.
Resolution	If conflict has occurred and people are upset, you need team tactics. **Visible:** One of the rules to have in your team charter is conflict must be visible to resolve it – it's okay if someone has upset you. **Role playing:** Role playing is useful, either after the situation or before a situation so people can learn how to handle it well. This is powerful to help people to learn what is triggering or how not to be triggered by someone else's misplaced words. **Good faith:** Resolution can only occur if both parties enter with good faith that they will both take an active role in resolution.

Watch your words	Good intentions and wrong words still cause problems.
	Using non-triggering language is a skill that needs to be learned.
	Accepting good intentions from others when angry is a skill also.

Crucial conversations*

Be genuine when asking others to share their facts and their perspectives. And listen, listen, listen. As they share, remember the skills of a good listener:

- **Ask:** Common invitations to share include, 'I'd really like to hear your opinion on ... ', and, 'Can you tell me more about that?'
- **Mirror (to confirm feelings):** Critical in this stage is your tone of voice. Share what you perceive. For example: 'I sense that you are angry ... ', or, 'You look unsure ... '
- **Paraphrase (to acknowledge their story):** Stay out of emotions and use their language as much as possible. Start with a phrase like, 'Let's see if I understand ... ' The area you most want to cover is the meaning they have put onto things.
- **Prime (when you are getting nowhere):** For those who put up walls, you might need to encourage them to speak by suggesting something you think they are thinking or feeling; for example, 'Do you think I'm being unfair?', or, 'I sense you are feeling misunderstood ... '

When	Situation	Principles and skills
Before	1. Results and relationships are suffering.	You need to hold a crucial conversation: • Identify where you are stuck. • Unbundle with CPR: content. pattern. relationship.

---

* For more on crucial conversations, check out *Crucial Conversations: Tools for talking when stakes are high*, second edition, by Kerry Patterson, Joseph Grenny, Ron McMillan and Al Switzler.

When	Situation	Principles and skills
Before cont.	2. You need to initiate a crucial conversation or one is evolving.	Start with heart: · Focus on what you really want – for you, them, the relationship, the organisation and long-term results.
	3. If you are getting emotional or telling clever stories.	Master your 'clever stories' – tell the rest of the stories. **Victim story:** What am I pretending to not notice about my role in the problem? **Villain story:** Why would a reasonable, decent person do this? **Helpless story:** What should I do now to move towards what I want?
	4. If you have a tough message, be honest and maintain safety.	State your path. Share your facts – 'I noticed twice you ...' Tell your story – 'I'm beginning to wonder if ...' Ask for others' paths – 'How do you see it?' Talk tentatively – own your story, avoid absolutes Encourage testing – 'Do you see it differently?'
During	5. Others are already in silence or violence and you missed the early warning signs.	Learn to look: · for the signs that a conversation is turning crucial · for early warning signs of silence and violence.
	6. If someone misunderstands your intent regarding purpose or respect.	Contrast: · I don't think/mean/want ... (their fear/misunderstanding). · I do think/mean/want ... (your actual purpose/meaning).

When	Situation	Principles and skills
During cont.	7. The discussion is going in circles. People are arguing. You are beginning a tough project or discussion.	**Mutual purpose** Create and commit to mutual purpose. 'Can we look for something that we both agree on?' **Recognise the purpose behind the strategy** 'Why do you want ... ?' 'This is why I want ...'
	8. If someone is going to silence or violence, then their meaning isn't getting into the pool.	**Explore other paths** Ask, mirror, paraphrase, mirror.
After	9. When you are ready to move to action.	Determine who, what, when and how.

Way forward

C – **Healthy conflict management** is all about giving people the tools and skills to handle conflict respectfully. Without this, there is no psychological safety. Learning this takes time and practice. This workout takes you one step closer to creating greater team cohesion, removing dysfunction to create a high-performance team

The next workout is **E – Energy multipliers and drainers**, which is about getting the team to recognise when they are drained and when they are feeling energised. It's also about recognising what causes these feelings and how they can learn to recognise the signs and know what actions need to be taken to replenish their team and their own personal energy batteries.

FACES – ENERGY MULTIPLIERS AND DRAINERS

Who

This workout is for you if the following is familiar to you:

· Your teams work at an unsustainable pace and are suffering fatigue and burnout.
· You are personally exhausted from your job.
· You team's performance is being impacted by negative energy.

What you will learn in this workout:

· How to manage your energy effectively.
· How to understand if you are bringing positive or negative energy to your team.
· How to recognise if your team's energy battery is full or empty.
· How to build the concept of energy into your team discussions.

Why

Teams with a flat battery

Identifying when teams are trending downwards with negative momentum is a complex task. However, spotting when a team's energy battery is flat and needs a recharge is critical to high-performance teams. As a leader you may not always have visibility on the extent of the problem and why a team's battery is flat. Burnout is common in the workplace, as is bad behaviour.

When a team's battery is flat they are at risk of people leaving, significantly impacting the equilibrium of the rest of the team. I am frequently disappointed at how much time and effort is spent hiring new team members, but there is not the same effort given to retaining team members. It is almost as if companies take the employee departures personally and don't want to talk about them.

The cost of people leaving is frequently 100% to 150% of their salary. People retention is a critical issue to high performance. The cost of people leaving is extremely high.[37]

Teams with a full battery

High-performance teams have full batteries and, as a consequence, can achieve more than teams with flat batteries. If you want to transform your energy, you need people and teams with full batteries. Transformations are tough going and a full battery is critical for success.

What

Energy has two components:

- personal, individual energy
- group energy.

It is important to reflect on both batteries and if they need a recharge and what impacts them. Energy naturally ebbs and flows. You cannot stop that, but it is important to discuss and recognise it so that everyone understands what action needs to be taken next – continue, or pause and recharge. A team or a person running on an empty battery is not useful to anyone.

Is your battery full or empty?

Reflect on a regular basis on how full your energy battery is, whether this week topped up your battery or if it reduced your energy supplies. Understanding what has a positive and negative impact on your energy battery is critical. Having frequent (weekly) discussions as a team about your personal and team batteries is a good conversation to introduce healthy balance into your teams.

Your personal impact on the team's energy battery

It is also super critical to reflect on your personal impact on the team's weekly performance and energy battery. Did you help increase the team's battery? Or did you drain it? If so, why and how? It is really important to consider how your behaviours and actions are impacting others. Most people do not spend enough time thinking about it, so are unaware if they are negatively impacting the group.

Things that drain a team's energy batteries

Some common negative impacts on people's energy batteries are:

· back-to-back meetings all day
· feeling unsupported or let down by others
· being overwhelmed with too much work
· all of the above combined.

Visualisation

The best way to get teams thinking about their energy is with visualisations. You can use two visualisations: one to represent the team's energy battery and the second to represent their personal energy battery.

Visualisation is used to encourage debate and discussion. Simply ask people to assess their own battery and the team's battery current energy levels from 1 to 5. Ask them to do it separately and then ask them to share. It is important to encourage debate and discussion. It is also helpful for people to realise there is no right or wrong answer.

Group discussion and trends

Ask the team to assess if both batteries are increasing with energy or decreasing this week compared to last week.

Multipliers and drainers

Ask people what has had a positive or negative impact on these batteries this week. Ask them if they think they are positively or negatively impacting on the team battery. Have a discussion as to whether the battery levels are sustainable, or if you need to do something different.

Personal impact

Ask each person to assess if they have personally increased the team's energy battery or depleted it and why. Ask them how they could personally increase the team's energy battery next week. What will they do to help recharge the team's battery?

Way forward

E – Energy multipliers and drainers as a workout is all about teaching people awareness of their own personal energy battery and the group's energy battery, and if it is empty or full and the best way to recharge it. This is a critical discussion because running a business transformation is like running a marathon – it takes time and you need to have something left in the tank at the end to finish it successfully.

The last workout for transforming behaviours to improve cultures is **S – Self-awareness**. This is perhaps the most important workout of all. It is about encouraging people to look inward at themselves and their own behaviour to identify what their strengths are that they can contribute with, and what areas are not strengths and need to be complemented by others. This workout also teaches people that strengths can be over or under developed, and how they can recognise when they are over or under using them. It also provides language for people when providing feedback to each other.

FACES – SELF-AWARENESS

Who

This workout is for you if the following is familiar to you:

- You and your team members are not aware of your strengths or how to activate them.
- Personal strengths and how to use them are not common discussions in the workplace.

- People are struggling to understand each other.
- People do not have the right language to anchor their feedback discussions with each other.
- People are too focused on others rather than reflecting on their own behaviour and impacts.

What you will learn in this workout:

- The power of positive psychology.[38]
- The benefits of focusing on your team's strengths rather than their weaknesses.
- What the 24 strength characteristics are and how to use them to communicate.
- How others rate against the 24 characteristics.
- Using self-assessment to identify your key personal strengths.
- How your personal assessment and someone else's may impact you both.
- How to develop a language to explain a situation and why it happened using character.
- How to encourage people to improve themselves first over improving others.

Why

Focus on strengths not weaknesses[39]

The best way to get the most out of yourself and your team is to focus on your strengths and not your weaknesses. I love this. It is super powerful. Everyone has natural inclinations and abilities and we need diversity of strengths – we don't need everyone to be good at the same things. So to build a high-performing team, focus on their strengths. Research from Yale, Gallup and the VIA Institute has proven the benefits of focusing on strengths.

The Gallup study has shown when employees focus on their strengths they feel more confident, are more self-aware and are more productive. This leads to higher employee engagement scores, greater retention of people and increased performance of teams. Our strengths are our greatest assets and should be leveraged for advantage.

Focusing on people's strengths also enables them to feel safe in their environment because they know they do not have to be perfect at everything. This gives them greater confidence to perform and instils an experimentation mindset, as people are less worried about failure because blame is not considered a problem in a strength environment.

What

So, how can you bring the power of positive psychology into your team and benefit from it for team cohesion?

Self-assessment

The VIA Institute is a not-for-profit organisation in Ohio. Their focus is the science of strengths and wellbeing. They offer a free 10-minute assessment to establish a person's strengths. I use this survey with all the teams I run. Everyone loves it, and it provides great language for us to focus on and learn from. Check it out at https://www.viacharacter.org/.

The great thing about this assessment is it gives people a language to use together. People frequently struggle with the right language for feedback situations.

Group discussion

Discuss in a group each other's strengths and how they impact the work you do as a team. Talk through real examples to bring them to life. Discuss if it is possible to have greater alignment of tasks associated with strengths.

Strength regulation[40]

Strength characteristics are like muscles in that they can be over or under developed. This is a good analogy to help people articulate how they feel or how someone makes them feel. Reviewing over or under developed strengths is a great discussion for teams.

This is less triggering language because you provide examples of where muscles are under developed and discuss how team members just need to build up certain muscles by applying exercises to these muscles, rather than using areas of improvements and weakness.

Strength collisions

Character strengths are dynamic, so our strengths can create positive or negative synergies with others. When a strength collision occurs, it's often the case that we perceive the other person's strength as a weakness. This occurs because we tend to consider our strengths as superior and absolute. We perceive our behaviour to be the 'right' way to deal with the situation at hand. Thus, strength collisions can be reduced when we are willing to step into the other person's shoes and see the situation from his or her perspective. Rather than looking at the other person's behaviour as a weakness, view his or her behaviour as a strength. In this way, both parties can take responsibility for their part, and the room is created to find a more harmonious expression of strengths.

Way forward

S – Self-awareness is the final workout of the behaviour-led cultural change. This last workout is all about getting people to focus on themselves rather than others, and gives people the language to provide feedback and deal with conflict. It also gives them useful language for discussing their strengths.

YOUR BEHAVIOUR MUSCLES ARE NOW FITTER AND STRONGER

If you want to lean into agility as an organisational capability, then people need to change. Behavioural change starts with you at the top. You must go first and role model for others what good behaviour is. Only then will your teams realise you are serious and the organisation is transforming. FACES is designed to help you rebuild your team so that you can avoid or reduce the five dysfunctions of a team. These are practices I have used over the years to build high-performing teams who deliver great outcomes.

Are you ready to turn your people into a high-performance team?

The last organisational muscle group to work is Mastery. This is all about giving people a structured path to organisational and team mastery and helping them realise that mastery takes time. There are practices that will help you achieve mastery – mastery is achieved with active doing not passive training.

CHAPTER 8

HOW — BUILDING A CONTINUOUS LEARNING ORGANISATION

'WHAT I HEAR, I FORGET;
WHAT I SEE, I REMEMBER;
WHAT I DO, I UNDERSTAND.'

CONFUCIUS

WHY WE NEED ORGANISATIONAL MASTERY

This chapter is about creating a self-learning, adapting and growing organisation and the best way to do that. If you want to transform your organisation into fast and adaptive, you need everyone to continuously learn, change and adapt, and to do that you need to give teams the right environment for this change to occur.

Path to mastery		Workout to move to next level
Unconscious incompetence (ignorance)	L1	Role model – observation
Conscious incompetence (awareness)	L2	Learn by doing – assisted
Conscious competence (learning)	L3	Learn by doing – unassisted
Unconscious competence (mastery)	L4	Role model for others

When organisations embark on a journey of transforming into a fast and adaptive organisation, they frequently underestimate how much work is involved in their teams and do not understand the best way for teams to learn how to do something new. This usually manifests itself in teams 'pretending' to understand what the change is, why they are doing it and what good looks like because they are actually unaware of what good is. Organisations ignore that learning happens in stages and people and teams can transition through these stages at different speeds.

Common mistakes organisations make when teaching teams new ways of working:

· Classroom training – primary learning approach that only has a 20% recall after one week.
· No role modelling – not showing teams what 'good looks like' so teams can't recognise it.
· No learning journey – not helping teams realise that learning is a multi-level journey to mastery.

- Inexperienced coaches – using coaches who have not achieved mastery.
- No learning by doing – not appreciating that practice has a 90% recall after one week.

This table clearly shows why classroom training is not enough and multiple practices are needed to embed mastery in your organisation.[*]

Training components	Skills attained	Transfer to job
Theory +	10%–20%	5%–10%
Demonstration +	30%–35%	5%–10%
Practice +	60%–70%	5%–10%
Feedback +	70%–80%	10%–20%
Coaching	80%–90%	80%–90%

THE FOUR STAGES OF COMPETENCE TO ACHIEVE MASTERY

In 1969, Matthew Broadwell designed the four stages of learning that everyone must go through to get to mastery:

- unconscious incompetence (ignorance)
- conscious incompetence (awareness)
- conscious competence (learning)
- unconscious competence (mastery).

---

[*] Adapted from Joyce & Showers 1981.

This workout series is all about giving teams a structured approach to organisational mastery along with the optimal practices to learn at each stage. It is about not only education but also helping people realise that mastery takes time.

We learn with this workout how you can build an organisation into a self-learning, adapting and growing organisation using a structured model to enable teams to self-rate and anchor against. Teams can move at their own pace; I frequently recommend six weeks minimum at each level of learning – so approximately 24 weeks to learn a new skill to mastery level.

The intent of this section is to give structure to how you can apply IMPACT and FACES in your organisation while building a structured, self-learning and growing organisation. Every team is encouraged to embrace and be proud of the part of the learning journey they are at – all of the stages are important. The intent here is to set expectations with teams and CEOs on how long it takes to become good at something.

Way

Incentives and rewards tied to learning for high performance

To encourage a learning organisation, I usually tie incentives and achievement badges to the teams, so that we can encourage them to feel proud for achieving a level on the way to mastery. Learning is the best behaviour to reward in an organisation instead of performance. It encourages people to work together and collaborate for success, which is the optimal way to achieve high performance. I also reward and recognise teams rather than individuals, also for cohesion and so I'm not encouraging people to feel they are better than others. We want everyone to succeed, not just individuals.

Digital badges for accreditation

I have frequently used websites such as Credly to set up multiple levels of learning, with badges and awards at each stage. Teams and people seem to like achieving badges because it provides a sense of accomplishment.

Enterprise-wide learning showcase and awards

I recommend having organisation-wide six-week showcases on learning to put the right level of attention onto it. Teams are awarded their badges here together and pick one best-in-class experience over the past six weeks. This is a fun way to set the right tone and culture on learning in an organisation.

Awards are set on the same rhythm for all teams. The CEO attends and presents the awards to show the importance of becoming a self-learning and growing organisation.

THE FOUR LEVELS OF LEARNING

Level 1 – Role model – observation (SEE IT)

We don't know that we don't know

Every team starts at level 1. There is no bypassing it.

Learning style for Level 1 – Role model – observation

For Level 1, passive classroom training is not enough. The critical enabler at this level is role modelling. For the skill or capability that you are learning, find a role model team who have done it already. Observe them in action and get them to share what worked and what didn't, and get them to show you what to do. If you have not seen something done well, how do you know how to recognise good? You don't. So you must observe and learn from a team who have mastered the skill.

Definition of role model:
- A team who has gone through all four levels of learning to achieve mastery.
- A team who are using the capability in their work practices and are excelling at it.
- A team who serves as a positive example of mastery of a capability or skill.

- A team who exemplifies the behaviour you want emulated in the organisation.
- A team who, if other teams were to imitate it, you would be happy.

Benefits of role modelling for both parties:

- Role modelling has a positive impact on both the master and the student groups:
  - **Mastery team** – teaching a skill to another team requires a team to think about what they do and why it works. It really helps cement a capability when you need to teach someone else to do it.
  - **Student team** – how can you learn a new capability if you have not seen what good looks like in a real-life work situation? To start the learning journey on the right foot, watching a team who excels at this capability is critical for success.

How it works:

- Timeframe – propose a three- to six-week engagement period for student and mastery teams.
- Classroom training – kickstart with knowledge training, where capability key points are identified.
- Observation – the intent is low effort for the mastery team as they are simply observed.
- Q&A – weekly check-ins and Q&A in a casual environment – even over beers and pizzas – to answer any questions that the students have.
- Student team start discussing weekly how they will implement in their work practice.
- Weekly check – mastery team validates student team against the capability key points weekly.
- Level 1 accreditation achieved if student team complete all the capability key points.
- Celebration time – every level achieved is celebrated! Teams should feel proud.
- Time commitment – up to four hours a week for student team over the period, and one hour a week for mastery team.

Way forward

Level 1 – Unconscious incompetence is mandatory for everyone. It is to help people realise that ego and confidence is greatest at this stage, so thinking that they don't need to do this level is exactly what this level of learning and mastery is all about! Remember there is no correlation between confidence and mastery. Observing someone or a team that has achieved mastery is a way of showing people what to aim for. It is about defining good before they start their own journey.

The next level is **Level 2 – Conscious incompetence**, which simply means watching someone perform at a mastery level and realising you are not that good and accepting that is okay. We are learning new skills, after all. This is where humility pops in.

Level 2 – Learn by doing – assisted (DO IT)

We know that we don't know

Knowing is not the same as understanding. Learning by doing is the key to accelerating change.

In level 1, the team has spent time observing and learning from a team that has mastered a skill. They should have the awareness to know they do not have the skillset yet. Here they learn that they are not competent at something. This often comes as a rude awakening.

Think about when you were learning to ride a bike or drive a car. You needed to practise. You learned with an instructor watching your moves, correcting actions and behaviours where necessary and staying with you until they were confident you had all the knowledge to be safe and had mastered the skill. This is the learning style for **Level 2 – Learn by doing – assisted**.

Learning style for Level 2 – Learn by doing – assisted

In level 1, the team worked with another team who role modelled mastery. Having observed them for a while and thinking about how to apply it to their way of working, the team need to be ready now to give it a go! However, at level 2 I recommend that this is still a 'supported journey', so bad habits don't creep in and the team can be course corrected quickly and easily. So level 2 is *learn by doing – assisted*, which means the team brings what they learnt into 'doing their work' and are supported by someone with 'mastery' experience

Definition of learn by doing – assisted:

Learn by doing is a simple idea – that we are capable of learning more about something when we perform the action. However, it is also wrapped in a prerequisite of observing mastery in action (level 1) and being assisted in doing (level 2), so your learning by doing is guided by someone who has achieved mastery in this skillset already.

> **'For the things we have to learn before we can do them,
> we learn by doing them.'**
> ## ARISTOTLE

Benefits:

- Knowledge retention is significantly higher than passive training.
- Being guided by someone with mastery as you 'do' means you get in-the-moment feedback.
- Applying the knowledge to the work you need to do allows you to understand its application.
- It increases team cohesion with community learning, where people are working and learning together.

How it works:

- Run as a six-week engagement.
- Understand as a group how the knowledge will benefit you.
- Create a hypothesis associated with the benefits of the knowledge.
- Define how you will measure success, baseline and track.
- Have a master-level coach observe you as you utilise the knowledge.
- Use weekly check-ins to see if it is delivering the required results or if you need to adapt.
- Showcase at the end – where you started, what you did, prove with evidence the results, make a recommendation for going forward.
- Reward and recognise publicly.

Way forward

Level 2 – Conscious incompetence is about humility. Having observed mastery in level 1, the team is now aware they are not at that level yet and they are okay with it. *Learning by doing – assisted* is the optimal learning pathway for this stage of mastery. You have observed mastery, so you are now putting it into practice, but you are still assisted so bad habits do not creep in.

The next workout for mastery is **Level 3 – Conscious competence**. The team has observed mastery, they have practised the skill for a while, so they are improving because they are using it in their daily jobs. They are now ready to try doing it unassisted but guided by metrics instead.

Level 3 – Learn by doing – unassisted (DO IT)

We work at what we don't know

Learning style for Level 3 – Learn by doing – unassisted

Having gone through level 1 and level 2, the team's confidence has grown and they are ready to ride their bicycle without its training wheels – or go solo! Repeatability is the key skill here. Effectively, this approach is the same as level 2, except that it is without a master coach observing, with the team upfront having agreed on the metric they are influencing for the period instead. So it is unassisted but measured, so they can assess if they are on or off track.

Definition of Learning by doing – unassisted:

- Level 3 is all about repeatability to ingrain the new practices.
- It is a repeat of level 2 without a master observing.
- It uses an agreed metric upfront as the 'guide' instead.
- The intent is to influence the metric from the start to the end.

Benefits:

- The intent is autonomy, ingrained with repeatability from level 2 and level 3.
- With autonomy comes confidence and solving problems without assistance.

- The process helps to teach and engage the team to use the metric as their guide.
- An evidence-based approach is highlighted as the way to success and embedding practices.

Way forward

Three workouts done; only one workout left to help you achieve mastery of a skill. The final stage to mastery is all about teaching someone else to do the skill. Only when you need to explain mastery to another person do you start to think about what it is that you do for success. It is also this final stage that builds the self-learning organisation. This approach is super powerful for creating the right culture because it is all about helping and assisting others.

Level 4 – Role model for others (TEACH IT)

We don't have to think about knowing it

In unconscious competence, the team has enough experience with the skill that they can perform it so easily they do it unconsciously. The final stage is where they've mastered the new practice or skill such that it is instinctual. They are no longer practising, but are still learning and growing. They have established a strong foundation and can be confident about their competency in this area. With competency comes humility; the team is comfortable not having all the answers, and appreciate the need for evidence over the need to listen to their own voices or opinions.

Learning style for Level 4 – Being a role model for others

Level 4 is about being the master role model for a team who are about to embark on level 1 of a new skill or practice. To be a master at a practice, a team *must* role model for others. Helping another team is what builds self-learning. It also sets the tone for the culture where teams help other teams get to mastery and autonomy.

Definition of being a role model:

- Level 4 and level 1 team create a plan that is evidence-based to start the journey to mastery.

Benefits of role modelling for others:

·   It sets the tone for culture as one of giving back and enabling other teams for success.
·   It enables a continuous self-learning and growing organisation to mastery.
·   It has a flywheel effect and enables the organisation to pick up pace in growth.
·   It sets the standard high for how to get to mastery – four levels are critical.

How it works:

·   Effectively this is the same as level 1 except the team who has recently mastered the skill is now the role model team.

Way forward

Level 4 teaching others mastery. The cultural benefits from this stage are massive. Also, this is all about continuous learning and growing that is self-driven by teams helping teams.

A CONTINUOUS SELF-LEARNING ORGANISATION

If you want your organisation to transform into fast and adaptive, you need to provide a structured way to achieve mastery in multiple practices and disciplines.

The key factors for success are:

·   Structured – four levels to mastery.
·   Equality – no team is allowed to bypass any stage; they may move more quickly but can't skip it.
·   Transparency – create mastery boards that are visible for all. (Make visible who has achieved mastery and for what, to help others understand who can assist their learning journey.)
·   Achievement focused and evidenced based – each practice is achieved with a metric to be influenced.
·   Culture – builds a culture of enabling and helping others.
·   Growth – it builds a continuous growth engine that adapts and learns continually.

This is when the power of a self-learning and growing organisation kicks in – teams who have learned mastery and are teaching other teams how to do it. The organisation becomes self-learning at this stage. Teaching teams to invest in the learning of other teams sets the tone in the organisation. They build relationships and then they are invested in other teams succeeding. This is where the true transformation occurs at scale, continuously.

AGILE CERTIFICATION PATH

Agile certifications have a place once you understand the context that they come under, which is when you have certified you are still at level 1, which is mandatory. And you need to go through the four levels to actually utilise the certification successfully. Certification is the start of a journey, not the end. If organisations go into the certification process with this frame of mind, there will be greater success. The biggest danger I see of certification is if the person, team and organisation assume it takes them to level 4 mastery, whereas it is actually just the starting point of level 1. Putting a newly certified person who has not achieved level 4 mastery in to coach a team is setting the organisation up to fail. It will embed bad habits that become hard to unwind, and increase the frustration of the organisation.

Obviously mastery should be hard to achieve – it is *mastery*. Do not downplay the skills, time, knowledge and experience to achieve it. Give it the respect it deserves.

CHAPTER 9
YOU <u>MADE</u> IT

'THE ILLITERATE OF THE 21ST CENTURY WILL NOT BE THOSE WHO CAN'T READ AND WRITE BUT THOSE WHO CANNOT LEARN, UNLEARN AND RELEARN.'

ALVIN TOFFLER

IS THIS THE END OF AGILITY?

Do not avoid the question

With people saying that 'agile is dead', don't have a knee-jerk reaction and take it literally. Listen to the message and understand why they are saying it. The question stands and it is a good, insightful question. Ignoring it and putting our heads in the sand will not make it go away. In fact, it will have the opposite effect and make the noise louder. The conclusion I have reached is this is more a 'trough of disillusionment' rather than an end. Agile is based on empiricism – a scientific, evidence-based process. We welcome the question and challenge because we want to make things better over being 'right'. We are so confident in our scientific approach that we encourage debate and believe in healthy conflict. The more evidence we collect, good and bad, the more we can optimise and increase chances of success for all. We are also aware that continuous improvement and adaption is ongoing as we face new and changing conditions daily. Embracing the question rather than ignoring it will enable us take a step change to the slope of enlightenment. That's what we want, right?

Learn to recognise it

If you are one of the 63% of organisations that has transitioned to agile or is in the process of transitioning to agile, then hopefully this book will give you the perspective you need to understand how to get success on your path forward and what pitfalls you need to watch for. We have spent time assessing and reviewing the agility masters so you can understand how other organisations have transitioned on their journey, so you can learn from them rather than copy them. This has given you the understanding of what good looks like and how to have greater success by being targeted with your agility tactics that can be custom designed to your organisation on the journey.

Build and strengthen your agility organisational muscles

On this journey, we have explored that agility is many things and that it is useful to consider the journey to be one of fitness and working on specific muscles for success. The muscle groups for organisation agility are:

- Outcomes – Outcomes first, fast and frequent
- Behaviours – Behavioural-led cultural change
- Mastery – A continuous self-learning organisation

Like all fitness journeys you need to complete a fitness test regularly, baseline where you are starting from and then apply workouts that will help you build and strengthen your muscles. Each workout targets a specific problem, and if you select the right workouts your ability to get quick success is high.

THE TIME FOR CHANGE IS NOW

The time has come to change your organisation. Now. Your organisational survival depends on it. Have you looked at your organisational health? Are you improving and getting fitter and heathier? How do you know? If you can't answer this question, the likelihood is your organisation is stagnating or going backwards and you are not even aware of it. Remember, revenue and profit are lag indicators. You need to track lead indicators. You need to move away from a fixed operational model to a constantly evolving operating model. Organisations are more representative of a living breathing system than a piece of machinery. Fast and adaptive is not achieved with a fixed or static way of doing things. You have realised in the digital age that a constantly evolving and adapting ecosystem operational model is the only path forward because it is flexible enough to deal with constant change without calling for a restructure every time you need to change and adapt to a business problem. Please note this does not mean the change is uncontrolled; that is simply chaos. What it means is that like a tree you can encourage and guide it to grow in a certain direction via the conditions you put it in. This is guided change through the chaos and complexity, not controlled and micromanaged.

LET'S GET STARTED

I hope you are feeling more confident about starting your business transformation, and your ability to use agility to make your organisation fast and adaptive. Like all fitness journeys the path forward is hard and requires discipline – anyone who tells you otherwise is a charlatan.

HOW IS YOUR RELATIONSHIP WITH AGILITY FEELING NOW?

I hope you are feeling more confident about your business transformation and going on a path to fast and adaptive. This book is designed to shine a light on the right path; you need to take that light and craft your own journey there. No one can do that for you.

The intent of this book is to address the noise head on relating to 'Is this the end of agility?' and to help everyone realise the question is a positive one that we can learn from and not a negative message. Fear and insecurity are the only reasons we would not lean into this question and welcome it.

In leaning into this question, the right level of awareness gets created to help everyone realise that a lot of organisations will fail on their agility journey and that you will need to go in with your eyes wide open so you don't become another market statistic. It is possible to sidestep some of the most common rollout problems, but you need to really understand what agility is before starting. This requires everyone to do some unlearning, to make space for relearning.

This book is designed to be thought provoking. The intent is to give you a jolt so you pay attention to the message. I want you to think about the why of your agility journey and find the urgency on why agility, fast and adaptive is critical. In doing so, I want to create a fresh appreciation that it is not one-size-fits-all or a silver bullet. If you have started this journey in your organisation and had previously failed, I hope this book has given you the confidence to recognise real agility and identify where you have gone wrong, and that you now have a plan in your head of an evidenced-based approach to fixing some of your issues. If you are about to embark on a fresh agility journey, I hope you realise that moving to quarterly planning, sprints and making everyone an agile coach will not give you agility, that there are better places to start for success, and you understand the importance of experience and mastery to help set up your organisation for success.

As you move forward with your agile transformation, I hope you will hold the question 'Is this the end of agility?' in your head at all times, as the reason it is asked is always relevant and should not be forgotten. Questioning, analysing and thinking critically about your path forward are essential for success. Blindly implementing what others have done is not.

Period of disillusionment

I have explored the question and reframed it instead to be a period of disillusionment rather than the end of agility, which means a rethink before plowing forward on your journey. It is important to realise that there are multiple paths forward – some will be successful, quite a lot will be negative. Hopefully knowing the common pitfalls to avoid will help you spot where others have gone wrong.

Slope of enlightenment

Copying another organisation will lead to failure in your approach. You must custom design your journey.

With the speed of change being accelerated by the age of digital, I am confident that fast and adaptive are critical enablers for all organisations for business success. However, hopefully you have learnt in this book that the path to fast and adaptive is littered with failures that are anything but fast and adaptive.

WHAT'S THE PATH FORWARD?

This book has provided a set of workouts for you to use on your business transformation to help you become fast and adaptive. There are some 'gotchas' along the way that can be avoided if you bring evidence and facts in, instead of opinions. However, you have everything you need in this book to equip you for your journey. How exciting. So, how do you tackle it and get started? The next pages will help you take that first step.

The journey to a fast and adaptive organisation starts here. It won't be 'done' in 12 months and is an ongoing journey, and it is a critical business enabler to stay relevant in a competitive marketplace.

I have created a 10-step process to 'ignite' your journey.

1. Be prepared/get ready

Understand where agility came from and why some people are shouting 'agile is dead'. Learn to recognise what agility is and what some of the most common pitfalls are that organisations fall into and how to avoid them, as well as understanding who the agility masters are and what they have done and why they are successful.

2. Find your WHY

You must have a WHY for starting the journey or you will fail. What is it? What problems are you expecting to solve? How will you know when they are solved? Does everyone recognise why you are doing this journey? This journey is hard with a high failure rate; if you don't find your WHY, when the going gets tough you will simply give up. So start with your WHY.

3. Take an agility FITNESS test

It is never wise to start any journey without assessing if you are in the right shape to start. What do you need to bring for the journey, how will you know if you are on the right path? What supplies do you need along the way? Are you fit enough to successfully complete it? If not, what areas do you need to focus on and what workouts will give you the required skills to build your strength and fitness to give you the greatest chances of success? Starting a journey without assessing your fitness will increase your failure rate.

4. Baseline your fitness

Most organisations are not fit enough to succeed on this journey yet. That is okay – it is good to recognise this rather than be foolhardy. Use the results from the fitness test to baseline your current fitness using evidence and data. This is your starting point, your baseline. These are what you are trying to improve on. This baseline is critical because it will help you prioritise what areas to focus on for greater success. It will also help you decide if what you are doing is improving you and making you fitter and stronger. Use the baseline to start tracking your trends.

5. Custom design your agility journey

The fitness test has identified which of the three muscle groups you need to work on as well as pinpointing which exact workout is required to strengthen and build your muscle. Use this baseline to choose which workouts you wish to implement in your organisation. The results from the fitness test and the carefully selected workouts will enable you to custom design your agility journey.

6. It is time to work out!

Like all fitness journeys, there comes a time when you simply need to do the hard yards. The workouts are it. Choose which workouts will make you fitter and stronger. Get started. You must validate that the workouts are giving you the required shift in strength – if not, do something different.

7. Build your OUTCOMES muscle group

If you have a weak Outcomes muscle group, choose from the six targeted workouts to make this muscle group. Achieve outcomes first, fast and frequent.

8. Build your BEHAVOURS muscle group

If you have a weak Behaviour muscle group, choose from the five targeted workouts to make this muscle stronger. Achieve behavioural-led cultural change.

9. Build your MASTERY muscle group

If you have a weak Mastery muscle group, turn your organisation into a self-learning, growing and adapting organisation by ensuring all teams and groups go on the four-stage journey to mastery.

10. Become an agility master

This is never achieved – you must constantly be adapting and evolving as an organisation for survival. So take regular fitness tests and work on your muscle groups. Remember, getting fit is hard work and so is maintaining it, but like all hard journeys the rewards are worth it.

It is time to get started! As CEO it is your responsibility to get involved. Agility is something that everyone needs to be involved in and is not something that your team does while you sit back and watch. Get involved to enable your organisation for success. Remove their road-blocks, and when the going gets tough, hold them on path.

WHO AM I?

I am an Irish female living in Melbourne, Australia, although I have worked in many cities across the global, including London, New York, Paris, Prague, Taiwan, Dublin and Milan. I have the joy and discomfort of never really truly fitting into an Australian culture due to my Irishness and femaleness, but it allows me to bring a different perspective to the problems at hand. I have learnt the skill of having to adapt to different geographical cultures and norms, frequently the hard way. My style is stereotypically Irish. I am searingly honest and outspoken, I am not afraid to challenge the status quo, I have a strong bias to decency and kindness to others as the only path to success and I believe work should be fun.

I am married and divorced and re-married, so I understand the feeling of failure from a work and a personal perspective, and how to recover from both. With teenage children, a rescue Great Dane and six turtles, I am comfortable and well equipped to deal with organisational chaos.

I am a lifelong long-distance runner and believe in the power of meditation to calm the noise. I have volunteered for many years in junior basketball in many roles at our local club – a club I vocally support because it is an inclusive basketball club and provides for all children regardless of ability or background, and it provides a pathway for young asylum seekers to join the club and feel welcomed and supported.

I firmly believe there is a better path to success where we accept that we do not have all the answers, but we simply choose to listen to our environment and genuinely adapt as we take the next step. How organisations are run and structured needs to change – we can do better. Let's just own it and change it.

PLEASE SHARE YOUR STORIES AND EXPERIENCES

Hopefully, you can feel my passion, energy and enthusiasm for transforming organisations into fast and adaptive! I love what I do! I hope it shows. This is my passion area. I would love to hear from you! Reach out, share your stories, your experiences, your frustrations. I love a good complex problem to deep dive with, and I am always happy to offer my time to assist and point organisations in the right direction!

Or perhaps your organisation is at agility mastery and you want to share your experiences of what worked, how you got there, and what pitfalls you fell into on the way. It is great to share stories and I am always curious and open about new ways of doing things and learning from others.

You can reach me at:

- www.linkedin.com/in/susanabishara
- www.sabishara.com (book me in for a 30-minute call).

DO YOU WANT TO SHARE MY ENERGY AT YOUR ORGANISATION?

If you have enjoyed reading this book, there are a number of ways that you can engage me from an organisational perspective.

SPEAKER – You need an inspirational speaker for an organisational event?

I present at conferences and organisations globally. I will bring a fresh, refreshing, funny take on topics, with the intent being to energise a group of people around action and seeing the future differently. Some topics I have presented recently:

- **Is this the end of agility?** – a 60-minute talk based on the contents of this book to revitalise your teams.
- **Accelerate time to value** – how flow can reduce your time to market by up to 50%.
- **Transparency at scale** – how transparency disappears when large organisations go agile and a case study on what we found when we put it back in.
- **Put the WHY back into your agility journey.**

Or I am happy to work with you to custom design a talk specifically for your organisation.

WEBINARS – You want to deep dive on some on the topics covered in this book and do Q&A?

I run limited attendees invitation-only webinars once a month which deep dive on sections of this book with practical tips on how to implement at your organisation and a focus on Q&A so that the audience can use the time to plan the best approach to introduce at your organisation.

AGILITY LEADERSHIP MENTORING – Your team have gone agile but you are unsure how to guide them?

We can book in for weekly and monthly executive coaching where I can guide and advise you on how to work with your team for agility success. This can be behind-the-scenes guidance, recommendations, spending time on your organisational challenges and providing expert guidance on tactics to resolve and improvement.

AGILITY FITNESS ASSESSMENTS – How agile are you? How should you custom design your journey?

If you are unsure where to start on your organisational agile transformation or simply want a second opinion, book me in to spend some time in your organisation. I will baseline your organisational agility today across over 10 different capabilities with a focus on baselining metrics and giving you a custom-designed agility journey for you to take forward.

The recommended approach is a three-month check-in to assess that progress is being made and is evidenced.

EMBED agility in your organisation plus role model

If you want to embed one or all three of the organisational agility muscle groups discussed in this book, I can come in and set up how to do it and stay with your teams until it is embedded and they are confident and autonomous. We can do this either as a short-term or a long-term engagement.

There is nothing I love more than working with a new team and guiding them on a journey for fast and adaptive. As mentioned in the book, the path to learning any new skill is getting someone with mastery experience to role model 'good' to others. This will set your team up for success with good practices and behaviours from the start

Purchase multiple copies of this book for your organisation

100% of profits of this book go to charities associated with women in technology. Purchasing this book and asking your team to think differently is a win immediately. As a female with a technology background, I am super passionate about contributing to representation of women in digital.

If you wish to buy in bulk please reach out for volume discounting. You can reach me at:

- https://www.linkedin.com/in/susanabishara
- https://www.sabishara.com (book me in for a 30-minute call).

RESOURCES

1   https://www.mckinsey.com/capabilities/people-and-organizational-performance/our-insights/the-organization-blog/8-ways-to-build-a-future-proof-organization

2   https://hbr.org/2021/11/todays-ceos-need-hands-on-digital-skills

3   'How to Create an Agile Organization', McKinsey, https://www.mckinsey.com/capabilities/people-and-organizational-performance/our-insights/how-to-create-an-agile-organization

4   https://www.mckinsey.com/capabilities/people-and-organizational-performance/our-insights/why-agility-pays

5   https://www.inc-aus.com/ilan-mochari/innosight-sp-500-new-companies.html; https://www.innosight.com/insight/creative-destruction

6   https://hbr.org/sponsored/2018/03/survey-data-shows-that-many-companies-are-still-not-truly-agile

7   https://www.scrumalliance.org/ScrumRedesignDEVSite/media/ScrumAllianceMedia/Files%20and%20PDFs/Learning%20Consortium/Learning-Consortium-for-the-Creative-Economy-Report-2015.pdf

8   https://www.forbes.com/sites/stevedenning/2019/08/23/how-microsoft-vanquished-bureaucracy-with-agile/?sh=49e3cc0f6f58

9   https://www.smharter.com/blog/how-large-successful-companies-achieve-agility-at-scale/

10 https://www.forbes.com/sites/kmehta/2021/03/09/the-future-of-innovation--how-microsoft-created-70000-innovators/?sh=2998117d5d4c

11 https://www.forbes.com/sites/stevedenning/2015/10/27/surprise-microsoft-is-agile/

12 https://rework.withgoogle.com/print/guides/5721312655835136/

13 https://rework.withgoogle.com/guides/managers-identify-what-makes-a-great-manager/steps/learn-about-googles-manager-research/

14 https://www.forbes.com/sites/jsimms/2022/05/31/japans-7-eleven-tycoon-bucks-the-trend-by-doubling-down-on-convenience-stores

15 https://www.slideshare.net/jocatorres/the-agility-paradox

16 https://asia.nikkei.com/Business/Retail/Seven-Eleven-Speedway-to-drive-record-profit-for-Japan-s-Seven-i

17 https://www.bosch-presse.de/pressportal/de/en/bosch-power-tools-sets-all-time-high-with-sales-of-5-8-billion-euros-in-2021-241280.html

18 https://www.wired.com/2013/04/linkedin-software-revolution/

19 https://www.forbes.com/sites/stevedenning/2016/11/26/can-big-organizations-be-agile

20 https://www.infoq.com/articles/agile-transformation-ericsson/

21 https://corporateagility.com/wp-content/uploads/2020/07/Benefits-of-Agile-Transformation-at-Barclays.pdf

22 https://www.amazon.com.au/Sooner-Safer-Happier-Antipatterns-Patterns-ebook

23 https://www.youtube.com/watch?v=3Ln9B-4toW0

24 https://www.youtube.com/watch?v=4GK1NDTWbkY

25 https://blog.crisp.se/wp-content/uploads/2012/11/SpotifyScaling.pdf

26 https://www.jeremiahlee.com/posts/failed-squad-goals/

27 https://www.jeremiahlee.com/posts/failed-squad-goals/

28 https://www.gao.gov/press-release/what-does-it-mean-be-agile-federal-government

29 https://www.forrester.com/blogs/adaptive-enterprises-are-growing-at-3x-faster-than-competitors/

30 'IT Portfolio Management and IT Savvy: Rethinking IT investments as a portfolio', MIT Sloan School of Management, Center for Information Systems Research, Summer Session, Peter Weill, June 14, 2007.

31 https://www.businessinsider.com/toxic-work-culture-job-advice-great-resignation-careers-2022-6

32 https://www.forbes.com/sites/forbeshumanresourcescouncil/2018/06/04/cronyism-the-one-not-so-obvious-mistake-that-can-destroy-company-culture/?sh=3732f5e76d92

33 https://www.ox.ac.uk/news/2019-10-24-happy-workers-are-13-more-productive

34 https://www.forbes.com/sites/forbescoachescouncil/2017/12/13/promoting-employee-happiness-benefits-everyone

35 https://www.inc.com/rhett-power/10-reasons-why-it-is-important-create-a-happy-workplace.html

36 https://www.forbes.com/sites/roncarucci/2017/03/14/how-to-use-radical-candor-to-drive-great-results/?sh=576c80524e23

37 https://www.afr.com/work-and-careers/careers/the-real-cost-of-losing-a-star-performer-20200217-p541go

38 https://positivepsychology.com

39 https://www.forbes.com/sites/forbescoachescouncil/2020/02/06/why-leaders-should-focus-on-strengths-not-weaknesses/?sh=6f1043b93d1a

40 https://www.viacharacter.org/pdf/Golden_mean_overuse_underuse__optimal_use_of_CS_(Niemiec_2019).pdf